JOSEPH ELMER
CARDINAL
RITTER

Joseph Elmer Cardinal Ritter

His Life and Times

Monsignor Nicholas A. Schneider
Foreword by **Justin Cardinal Rigali**

Liguori
LIGUORI, MISSOURI

Imprimi Potest:
Thomas D. Picton, C.Ss.R.
Provincial, Denver Province
The Redemptorists

Published by Liguori
Liguori, Missouri
www.liguori.org

ISBN 978-0-7648-1701-4

Liguori Publications, a nonprofit corporation, is an apostolate of the Redemptorists. To learn more about the Redemptorists, visit Redemptorists.com.

Printed in the United States of America
11 10 09 08   4 3 2 1
First edition

Dedicated to Donald and Nancy Ross,
whose generosity led to its publication.

Contents

Foreword

Joseph Elmer Cardinal Ritter faithfully guided the Church of St. Louis in an era of momentous change. Monsignor Nicholas Schneider's biography, *Joseph Elmer Cardinal Ritter: His Life and Times*, gives the reader an insight into the man and the times in which he lived. From Cardinal Ritter's early days in Indiana and his ordination as a priest and bishop in Indianapolis, Ritter was recognized early as a gifted pastor and administrator. He was a man ahead of his times in his advocacy of racial desegregation in both Indianapolis and St. Louis. Despite resistance, Ritter pastorally and authoritatively desegregated St. Louis' Catholic schools in 1947, several years before the famous Supreme Court decision in *Brown v. Board of Education of Topeka* did the same in the public schools. Ritter was among the first to establish a diocesan mission in South America, predating the call of Vatican II for bishops to aid the world's missions. Finally, Cardinal Ritter was outstanding among the American bishops during Vatican II, especially with the so-called American document of the Council, *The Declaration on Religious Freedom*. Ritter was also a strong advocate of the Council's endorsement of ecumenism and interreligious relations and the renewal of the liturgy. Monsignor Schneider's biography captures the fascinating role of Cardinal Ritter faithfully serving the Church during a revolutionary time in American church history. As a former successor of Cardinal Ritter in St. Louis, I willingly commend this book to the public.

Justin Cardinal Rigali
January 7, 2008

Introduction

Joseph Elmer Cardinal Ritter, who died on June 10, 1967, was among the most important prelates of the twentieth-century American Catholic Church, yet no comprehensive account of his life has been written. This book is an attempt to correct that omission. It is composed without footnotes and is designed to be read, not so much as an account of history, but rather as a narrative of events in the life of a distinguished churchman. In telling his story, I have relied heavily on the cardinal's correspondence and speeches, which are prime sources for discovering his state of mind at any given time. Around these are woven the tale of events that shaped and readied him to positively affect the affairs of his day.

Cardinal Ritter had several "firsts" to his credit as a bishop:

+ He was the first to desegregate an entire diocesan school system.
+ He was the first to host three National Liturgical Weeks.
+ He was the first to send diocesan priests as missionaries to South America.
+ He was the first to build a diocesan hospital dedicated solely to the health care of children.
+ He was the first to give a major address at an American Protestant seminary.

These achievements alone justify a biography, but his story is rich in many other ways. He was totally dedicated to his vocation; had a broad pastoral sense; demonstrated a willingness to fish in the deep waters of ecumenism, social justice, and Catholic education; and was a participant in Vatican Council II. Even his sense of humor, which helped him keep his balance in trying times, helped make him the shepherd-leader who served the Church brilliantly and selflessly over many years in so many ways.

The information used for this biography was gleaned primarily from the archives of the Archdioceses of Indianapolis and St. Louis and those of St. Meinrad Seminary, as well as the main public library of New Albany, Indiana. I am grateful to the head archivist of the St. Louis collection, Audrey Newcomer, and two of her assistants, Helen Gollihur and Elaine Snyder, for their untiring response over many months to my requests; to Jane Newland, assistant archivist of the collection in Indianapolis, for her courtesy and assistance; to Lois J. McEntarfer, Registrar and Director of Institutional Research of St. Meinrad School of Theology, for locating information regarding the cardinal's academic career at that seminary; and to the pastors and staffs of St. Mary of the Annunciation Parish in New Albany and the Cathedral Parish of Saints Peter and Paul in Indianapolis for their help in obtaining information from their sacramental records. Finally, thanks to Helen Ritter of the family for her advice.

Special thanks go to Dr. Marie Kremer of St. Louis for her persistent correction of my typing mistakes and her suggestions to make the manuscript more readable. Any errors that remain are due to my oversight alone and for them I take full responsibility.

Finally, I thank Archbishop Raymond Burke for his permission to undertake this project and his encouragement in pursuing it.

Monsignor Nicholas A. Schneider
Thanksgiving Day
November 23, 2006

Publisher's Statement

This work of Monsignor Nicholas Schneider represents the first-ever attempt to weave together the major threads of Cardinal Ritter's life and ministry and present a broad overview of his significant accomplishments. It does not dig deeply into any one area of his ministry but presents an overview of his challenges and accomplishments, thus giving readers a glimpse into his local, national, and international influence. Throughout the book the author references Ritter's personal correspondence, passages from his talks, newspaper coverage, and so forth. Adding these individual moments together tells us of a bishop who struggled with potentially divisive questions, such as desegregation of the parochial school system, the Church's relationship to non-Catholic Christians and the Jewish and Muslim communities, and the principle of religious liberty.

In telling the Cardinal's life, the author may have overlooked, or did not have access to, information that would have helped tell more of the story. He would appreciate any corrections or clarifications, all of which can be sent to the publisher and will be forwarded to Monsignor Schneider to be considered for inclusion in a future edition of this book.

Liguori Publications thanks Monsignor Schneider for telling us the story of this modern churchman's life and times.

1

Welcome to St. Louis
The Early Years

SAINT LOUIS: CELEBRATION AND TRAVAIL

On that first Monday in October when Archbishop Ritter arrived in St. Louis, he was fresh from a retreat at Jesuit House in West Baden, Indiana. He came after years in Indianapolis, serving both as bishop and archbishop. He was rested and in his usual good humor, looking forward to his new task. Not surprisingly, he found St. Louis in celebration. They were not, however, celebrating the arrival of their new archbishop. After all, the life of St. Louis was and is baseball, and that October 7, the Cardinals were facing the Red Sox in the second game of the 1946 World Series.

Undoubtedly with a twinkle in his eye, the archbishop apologized to the delegation of civic and church leaders who met him at Union Station for having arrived at such a busy time. And busy it was: between the World Series and the Veiled Prophet parade, the archdiocese was compelled to forego an expected formal civic reception.

Though the life of the city was not the life of the church, Archbishop Ritter still jumped immediately into a whirlwind of activity. At 4:30 on the afternoon of his arrival, he met with the diocesan consultors to present to them the apostolic bulls directing him to take possession of the archdiocese. That evening the visiting archbishops and bishops were hosted for dinner at the Cathedral rectory.

TERMINOLOGY

apostolic bull

An *apostolic bull* or a *papal bull* is a special type of communication issued by a pope. The name is derived from the seal *(bulla)* affixed at the end to authenticate it. Practically speaking, an apostolic bull is an apostolic letter that has a leaden seal. A bull could deal with a range of topics, including excommunications, statutory decrees, episcopal appointments, dispensations, canonizations, apostolic constitutions, and convocations. In earlier times, all papal letters were referred to as *bulls;* today a papal bull is issued only for the most formal or the most solemn of occasions such as the appointment of a bishop.

The morning of his arrival, every parish in the diocese had offered a Solemn High Mass, asking God's blessings on the archbishop through the intercession of Our Lady of the Rosary, the feast of the day. Religious communities provided all-day exposition of the Blessed Sacrament, closing with a holy hour for the same intention.

The following morning, October 8, the new archbishop of St. Louis was enthroned at the Cathedral, the first bishop so enthroned in the ninety-nine–year history of the archdiocese. When the first archbishop, Peter Richard Kenrick, was appointed in 1847, he received the pallium from his brother, Francis Patrick Kenrick, bishop of Philadelphia, who brought it from Rome, having received it from Pope Pius IX. Kenrick's successor was his coadjutor, John J. Kain, who was in turn succeeded by his coadjutor, John Joseph Glennon. Due to these circumstances, none of them had been enthroned.

TERMINOLOGY

pallium

The *pallium* is a small woolen circular band given by the pope to an archbishop who oversees bishops caring for dioceses within a fixed area. It is a symbol of his participation in the supreme pastoral power of the papacy and conceded to him for the geographical region of which he is the metropolitan archbishop.

Low Mass

A Mass celebrated by a priest alone with a server(s); a shortened and simplified form of a High Mass.

Solemn or High Mass

The full ceremonial form of the Tridentine Mass, celebrated by a priest with a deacon and a subdeacon, with most of the parts of the Mass sung, and with the use of incense. Priests often take the parts assigned to the deacon and subdeacon.

Solemn Pontifical Mass

A *Pontifical High Mass*, also called *Solemn Pontifical Mass*, is a Solemn or High Mass celebrated by a bishop using certain prescribed ceremonies. For example, the bishop celebrates almost the entire first half of the Solemn High Mass (until the Offertory) at the *cathedra* (often referred to as his throne) to the left of the altar.

A *Pontifical Low Mass* was celebrated by the bishop but was spoken, not sung.

At the Solemn Pontifical Mass, Most Reverend Amleto Cicognani, the Apostolic Delegate, presided. Archbishop James H. Ryan of Omaha preached and said of Ritter: "He is a humble man, but he is solid because of his very humility. He is a kindly, considerate man. He is approachable by all. He is an excellent administrator. He is friendly to those outside the faith. He will be

ecum.

interested in the welfare of your beautiful city. He is, last of all, *a homo Dei* (man of God) in the best meaning of that term."

In his own remarks, Archbishop Ritter said:

> *We give ourselves to you, dearly beloved of the faithful, readily and entirely…While we willingly dedicate ourselves to this appointed task and know that God's help will not be wanting, nevertheless we realize the great need we have of your cooperation. We sincerely ask this, not only of the clergy, and religious men and women of the archdiocese, but also of the laity.*

So on that day, Archbishop Ritter assumed the care of St. Louis City and County and forty-three other counties in eastern Missouri. Included were 450 diocesan priests and 450 religious order priests, in addition to 4,000 sisters and brothers of 74 religious communities, all of whom served 650,000 laity in 307 parishes and missions.

Archbishop Ritter quickly learned that St. Louisans were loyal sports fans, especially of the St. Louis Cardinals baseball team.

St. Louis had served as the "Gateway to the West" for many religious communities, and a large number had established provincial headquarters or motherhouses in or near the city. Their presence was a great benefit to the diocese, both through works of charity and in education.

Ritter was a man of few pretensions and simple in his tastes, but he also needed a place away from the demands of his day, a place where he could indulge in his primary form of relaxation, gardening. So it is not surprising that he moved from downtown to a more private, quiet place, despite initial news reports concerning his intentions.

In fact, in an interview shortly after he arrived, Ritter told reporters that he intended to live in the archbishop's residence at 4510 Lindell Boulevard, a home purchased for the diocese in 1924 by Archbishop Glennon, who moved there to be closer to the Cathedral. However, in April 1947, St. Louis newspapers reported that negotiations were in progress for the purchase of a home on Ladue Road for archdiocesan purposes. When questioned about it, Monsignor John Cody, the chancellor, said that the archbishop would continue to live at the Lindell location. However, he did not discount the possibility that he might make the Ladue property his residence at some future date. The ten-room house, built about 1927, included three acres of land and was purchased for about $80,000.

On June 13, 1947, Ritter wrote to Archbishop Ryan of Omaha, "I am sorry that I forgot to mention about the house. I have a nice place and am gradually getting it furnished and prepared for occupancy...." Everybody seemed pleased about the move. He moved in later that summer.

On November 20, he wrote to an Indianapolis friend, Elmer A. Steffen, who owned a summer cottage Ritter used at Culver, Indiana: "It has been a busy Fall for me and I have not even gotten in all of my tulip and jonquil bulbs...I hope after the first of December, when there will be a let-up in my engagements, that there will be a little dry weather which will permit me to plant."

His decision to move to the county and live alone—except for a housekeeper, and a groundskeeper and his wife to look after things—proved to be a good one. He liked the solitude of the location in Creve Coeur and insisted that he lived "on Ladue, not in it," since Ladue was quite upscale by then. He had a statue of Mary, designed especially for him, in the garden, his favorite place for relaxation. The hoe he used had belonged to his grandfather, who had used it on his farm in Indiana a century before. In the hothouse he grew tomatoes, cabbage, radishes, and lettuce. He and his groundskeeper grew fresh vegetables throughout the year. He took special delight in having fresh tomatoes on Christmas Day.

Archbishop Ritter's simplicity and unpretentiousness led to some amusing incidents. Shortly after arriving, he began a tour of the rural areas. Pastors were notified of his coming, but one, with a faulty telephone connection, did not receive all the information. In addition, the archbishop was late, arriving about nine o'clock in the evening at the rectory where he was to stay the night. The pastor, perhaps reasonably, assumed Ritter had already eaten dinner, so he invited him to sit and relax. They talked for about an hour and, although he had had nothing but a sandwich since breakfast, the archbishop said nothing about his hunger. Before retiring, the priest offered him a snack of milk, cheese, and crackers. Only years later did he learn that he had sent his archbishop to bed hungry.

Later, still before he was well known in the city, he was puttering in the garden on a Saturday afternoon. Dressed in some old slacks, he was hard at work clipping a hedge when he was interrupted by a woman who drove her car up the driveway. She asked if the archbishop of St. Louis lived there. He told her he did. So they chatted for a time about the new archbishop, after which she finally drove off, blissfully unaware. And the new archbishop went back to clipping the hedge.

Monsignor Charles Helmsing described Ritter as having "ample good humor, a propensity to smile broadly and frequently, and a direct, sincere manner of speech which is not that of an orator but that of a conversationalist. His simplicity is evident in his quiet deportment and in an obvious aversion to rich costumes and lavish display."

EARLY EVENTS AS ARCHBISHOP OF ST. LOUIS

Health

With his smile and his good humor and simplicity, the life of the archbishop was not all sunshine and roses: similar to many of us, he had health concerns (he smoked cigars), which seem not to have been serious, though we have few details. On January 4, 1947, he wrote to Reverend Henry Herman of Indianapolis: "I have had a touch of my old trouble before the holidays and a recurrence since then. This prompted the doctor to send me to the hospital to make a complete test, similar to the ones made in Indianapolis. I hesitated to go but decided I would have to sooner or later if I was to satisfy the local doctors. Nothing was found and the tests tally perfectly with those of the hospital in Indianapolis."

The same day he wrote to Sister Andrea of St. Vincent Hospital in Indianapolis to thank her for sending information on his condition from there to DePaul Hospital where he was a patient.

> The report from St. Vincent's reached Doctor Kramolowsky yesterday. He was very glad to have it and his findings tally perfectly with those of eleven years ago. There seems, therefore, nothing to be worried about other than keeping myself in condition to avoid these attacks. They seem to be due to a cold and I suppose I must be more careful in avoiding drafts and keeping myself dressed a bit warmer.

Growing Pains

Archbishop Ritter determined very early that more funds would be needed to respond to the changes facing the diocese. In 1949, as Easter Sunday drew near, he sent word to the pastors that the Easter collection in parishes would have to be sent to the chancery. This would be used to assist poorer parishes and to build churches, schools, and other institutions. In addition, each parish would be assessed an amount to be met through the Easter collection or from regular parish funds.

This was met with consternation by many priests; for twenty years the Easter collection had been used to pay priests' salaries and take care of the household expenses. Not only were they losing a major source of their own income, but they recognized that the archdiocese was beginning to draw significantly from their parish financial resources to be used for nonparochial purposes. They were concerned that the money generated by their people would no longer meet the costs of providing the educational, and other, services to which people were accustomed. Nevertheless, though the directive met with great reluctance, it was highly successful. Between 1950 and 1955, the archdiocese spent $48,500,000 on its building program.

Archbishop Ritter was a friend of contemporary church art. He supported its incorporation into churches built during his tenure in St. Louis, among them the Church of the Resurrection in south St. Louis, St. Peter in Kirkwood, St. Clare of Assisi in Ballwin, St. Martin des Porres in Hazelwood, and St. Ann in Normandy, all of them new ventures in form and furnishings. The buildings caused some controversy, but all survived the test of time. He always personally approved drawings for buildings planned for any parish and would not allow more to be spent than he deemed the right amount. Archbishop Ritter is shown here at the groundbreaking for St. Peter Church in Kirkwood, which was completed in 1953.

The Postwar Challenges: Race, Education, and Immigration

With the end of World War II and the return of many thousands of men from military service to begin new lives and families, there was a major population shift to the suburbs of St. Louis. Money for building new high schools, accumulated during Glennon's ascendancy, had been dedicated prior to Ritter's arrival. While he was chancellor, Bishop Cody had conducted a drive that raised an additional three million dollars for this purpose. But though we shall learn more of the challenges of education, it was a small issue compared to the problem of segregation.

RACE RELATIONS

When he arrived in St. Louis, Archbishop Ritter showed a special interest in St. Joseph's High School, the Catholic high school for black students. At a dinner he attended there one evening, he learned that, although all other diocesan high schools were graduating their students at the Cathedral, St. Joseph's students were still graduating from St. Ann's Parish, where the school building was located. He ordered that changed and St. Joseph's graduates joined the others at the Cathedral in June 1947.

Foreshadowed by this action, his real goal was to integrate all parishes and schools of the archdiocese. He visited St. Joseph's High in March of 1950 and promised the students and faculty a new school building, since they were using the former St. Ann grade school. Sister Adelaide, the principal, reminded him of this in her letter thanking him for the visit: "Your promise of a new school was received by all of us with the greatest happiness; and knowing that you are a man of your word, no one doubts that the new school will be a reality." However, he thought better of it and by the end of the year had decided that full integration was the answer, not "separate but equal." St. Joseph would be closed and the students would be encouraged to enroll in one of the other diocesan high schools.

The *St. Louis Argus*, the leading black newspaper in St. Louis, carried an article on December 15, 1950, announcing the closing of St. Elizabeth Parish, noting the decision to do so "was reached by Archbishop Joseph E. Ritter in his desire to abolish any 'colored' church as such in the diocese." In a letter dated December 29, 1950, Monsignor William Drumm, the Chancellor of the archdiocese, informed the members of St. Elizabeth that the parish would close as of January 1, 1951, and directed them to join St. Malachy, St. Nicholas, or St. Bridget parishes. The *St. Louis Register* of January 12, 1951, reported, "Archbishop Ritter, in his desire to care for the greatly increased numbers of Colored Catholics in the archdiocese, and in keeping with the traditional practice of the Church in recent years, indicated to the reverend pastors his wish that the Colored families, which are now scattered throughout the city, should attend the territorial parish in which they are actually residing."

A Long Tradition

Separation of races had long been a fact of life in Missouri. Under the terms of the Missouri Compromise of 1820, by which the state was admitted to the Union, Missouri had the right to form a constitution and government without restrictions on slavery. In fact, slavery was not officially prohibited in Missouri until December 18, 1865, at the ratification of the thirteenth amendment to the U.S. Constitution, which abolished the practice.

During the Civil War St. Louis was divided, with half or less favoring the North and the rest the South. The city depended on the Mississippi River for its business and trade and this gave it an intimate connection with the South. A strong minority had strenuously sympathized with the Southern cause, and keeping the races separate was still a goal in the minds of many a hundred years later.

After his installation, Archbishop Ritter's first public appearance was at a Clergy Conference on "Negro Welfare" at Visitation Parish on October 16, 1946. There he learned that there were only 400 blacks among the 58,000 students enrolled in parochial schools in St. Louis. Further, he discovered that Visitation was one of only two archdiocese parochial schools admitting black children; the other was St. Elizabeth of Hungary—staffed by Jesuit priests. St. Elizabeth was the fourth parish in the United States founded for black Catholics. Its boundaries included the entire city of St. Louis. There was also a chapel of St. Clement for black people, sponsored by the Redemptorist Fathers in connection with their parish of St. Alphonsus Liguori, popularly known as the "Rock Church."

Nothing New Under the Sun

The matter of racial segregation was a familiar one for Ritter, who had faced deeply entrenched segregation in Indiana. While bishop of Indianapolis, he had initially followed the example of his predecessors by requiring Catholics to send their children to parish schools. Parents who disobeyed were threatened with the denial of the sacraments, a penalty applied in individual cases by Ritter and the bishops who served before him.

Bishop Ritter considered African-American children to be among the most neglected groups in the Indianapolis diocese. Racial inequality was widespread, and the Ku Klux Klan was a force to be reckoned with. David C. Stephenson, the Klan's Indiana leader, blatantly declared himself to be the law in the state. Klan members actively aroused bigotry and hostility to the Church.

The bishop had an intense concern for social justice, especially as it applied to black Catholics. He built a church for them, established a cultural center and five summer schools for catechetics, and quietly integrated the parochial schools.

In 1937, he ordered the integration of three girls' academies in the diocese. Two years later he instructed a grade school at the Beech Grove parish to admit black children. The protests that followed were so serious that he threatened to shut down the church and school. In 1942 he ordered integration of the Catholic high schools in Evansville. He ruled that any child of any race had to be accepted in any Catholic school and that all children had to wear uniforms so that the poor would not feel badly dressed.

Finally, in 1943 he integrated the Indianapolis archdiocese schools by decreeing that all children, regardless of color, could attend Catholic grade and high schools, provided they were equal to the work and able to pay the tuition. Some parents protested and others took their children out of the schools, but there was little public controversy and no organized resistance. The policy was still in effect when he left the diocese in 1946.

St. Louis: A Challenge

St. Louis was different. Segregation was a deeply entrenched part of life in the "River City." Daily life—including restaurants, movie theaters, hotels, banks, grocery stores, parks, swimming pools, neighborhoods, and, of course, churches and schools—was organized along color lines. Whites and blacks did not associate politically, socially, or religiously. While all were free to ride the public streetcars, even there an unstated but definite line was drawn concerning where riders could sit. It was as though two societies lived juxtaposed to each other, separate but certainly not equal.

Then, on September 26, 1946, the *St. Louis Register* carried an article stating that Cardinal Glennon had for some years in individual cases recommended admission of black students into elementary schools and high schools. Archbishop Ritter found in the cardinal's files a letter that directed some parish schools to admit black pupils. After some months of analyzing the situation, in the spring of 1947 he received two requests that caused him to act.

The first came from the director of the archdiocesan high schools, who was faced with overcrowding at St. Joseph's High School. He asked whether black students could be admitted to other high schools. Ritter replied that he had no right to refuse admittance to any diocesan high school provided the student applying was able to fulfill the scholastic and other requirements.

The second request came from Father John Smith, pastor of Visitation Parish, whose school had admitted both white and black children for several years. He determined that in September he would be faced with overcrowding and insufficient teaching sisters. He suggested that children living outside the parish boundaries might attend their respective parish schools. Ritter directed him to tell the parents of such children to have them attend school in their own parishes. About 150 students entered schools as far away as the Cathedral, St. Gregory in St. Ann Village, and St. Mary Magdalen in Brentwood. Furthermore, during the summer of 1947 he sent a letter to all pastors instructing them to end segregation practices in their schools before the 1947–1948 school term commenced.

The archbishop was not the first to tackle Catholic school integration in St. Louis. On February 11, 1944, Father Claude Heithaus, S.J., gave a sermon at a student Mass at Saint Louis University. He asked why black Christians, even if Catholic, could not attend the university, when Muslims and Hindus could. After explaining the Church's teaching on the Mystical Body of Christ, he asked the students to rise and pledge that they would work to prevent further injustice to blacks. The entire congregation took the pledge.

Father Patrick J. Halloran, S.J., newly appointed president of the university, objected to the sermon and ordered Hiethaus to keep silent on the matter of race. Heithaus appealed to the Missouri provincial, Father Joseph P. Zuercher, who encouraged Halloran to integrate the school, though he was upset with Heithaus. In the summer session of 1944, the university admitted five black students. Because of criticism and fears regarding equality and intermarriage, blacks were not allowed to attend the prom in 1945. Heithaus was later reassigned to Creighton University in Omaha.

Opposition and National Attention

Unlike in Indiana, when it became known that Ritter had ordered the integration of the St. Louis diocesan schools, opposition was brisk and forceful. On September 11, about 500 people from twenty-three parishes met at the Electrical Workers' Hall at 4249 Gibson Avenue. After much discussion two men were selected to call on the archbishop and request that he reverse his decision. They were directed to report back at a meeting in the same hall on Sunday night, September 14. Flyers were distributed at many Catholic churches that Sunday inviting parishioners to attend and noting, "At this meeting we expect to have an answer from Archbishop Ritter regarding the negro [sic] attending the Catholic schools…It is the Duty of Every Catholic in St. Louis and Vicinity to attend this meeting."

Some families had already transferred their children from parochial to St. Louis public schools, which were segregated. Black children were not admitted to public schools where whites were enrolled. During the September 11 meeting, the treasurer of the dissident group was applauded when he said, "If His Excellency the Archbishop wants schools for negro children, we will help build them, but we do not want colored and white children together in the schools, and we will not have it."

Sunday night saw an overflow crowd of 700 with more standing outside. A collection of $400 was taken from the group that claimed to represent forty-three parishes, the money to be used to finance an injunction suit against the archdiocese. Three people who spoke against the injunction were asked to leave. A twelve-member executive committee was formed to confer with a lawyer. The motion to retain legal counsel was made by a man who had two children in Saints Mary and Joseph School, a school that now had black students.

Ritter heard about the threatened legal injunction while on a confirmation tour in Perryville, Missouri. He immediately called the chancery office and dictated a letter to be read in all of the parishes on the following Sunday, September 21:

To the beloved Clergy and beloved Laity of the Archdiocese of St. Louis. Greetings!

It has come to our attention that a small group of individuals have signified their purpose of taking legal action to restrain us from carrying out a policy which we consider our right and duty as chief pastor of the faithful of this Archdiocese, regardless of race or nationality.

We realize that many of these good people are being gravely misled.

Consequently, we take this occasion to remind them of their filial obligation as Catholics to cooperate with the Bishop and Clergy and their fellow Catholics in issues which are fundamental in our holy Catholic Faith, namely, not only the equality of every soul before Almighty God, but also obedience to ecclesiastical authority.

After mature deliberation, and fully confident of the loyalty of the faithful, we now deem it opportune to caution them publicly. By the general law of the Church, there is a serious penalty of excommunication, which can be removed only by the Holy See. This penalty is incurred automatically should an individual or group of individuals, without permission, in violation of Canon 2341, presume (that is, with full knowledge) to interfere in the administrative office of their Bishop by having recourse to any authority outside the Church.

We hereby direct that this letter be read at all the Masses on this Seventeenth Sunday after Pentecost and the Feast of St. Matthew, September 21st.

Faithfully yours in Christ, Most Reverend Joseph E. Ritter, Archbishop of St. Louis.

Dated at the Chancery Office, September 20th, 1947.

That Sunday evening the protesting group, now known as "The Catholic Parents' Association of St. Louis and St. Louis County," met at a larger venue, St. Louis House, on Jefferson and Lafayette Avenues in midtown St. Louis. A resolution was passed to write to the Apostolic Delegate in Washington. The author of the letter was quoted by the *St. Louis Globe-Democrat* as saying, prior to the meeting, "I personally will not take any action that will jeopardize my religion or that of anyone else. We feel we have been within the laws of the Church so far and want to stay there." He told the people assembled that he had been informed by attorneys that an injunction to prevent blacks from attending Catholic high schools could not be obtained because the archbishop had full legal control of the schools. Nevertheless, feelings continued to run high. One Catholic mother wrote to the *St. Louis Post-Dispatch:*

> *I am a Catholic mother of three small children who will soon begin to attend a Catholic school. We, the Catholics who are objecting to Archbishop Ritter allowing the Negro children to attend our schools with white children, are not just a small minority of 500. This number attending the three recent meetings were merely a representative delegation of over 50,000 people. The hall available was not big enough to hold all the people of the 47 parishes represented. We have no desire to see our children intermarry with the colored race. Association and intermingling of white and colored children from grade school on would inevitably lead to this."*
>
> *Worried Mother*

A *Newsweek* brief published on September 29, 1947, described the Most Reverend Joseph E. Ritter as being in a "bitter fight with some 700 of his parishioners." And the *St. Louis Register* of October 3 carried a picture of Ritter taken the week before at the consecration of Bishop Hubert M. Newell in Denver. He looked strained and did not have the usual humor in his eyes. Clearly the confrontation over the school issue weighed heavily on him.

On Sunday, September 28, the objecting group met at St. Louis House to sign petitions in protest against the admission of black students to Catholic schools. The text had been framed at a meeting the night before. The stated purpose was to "demonstrate to the archbishop that we are not a minority as he stated in the official Catholic newspaper, the *St. Louis Register*...We hope by showing the archbishop the sentiment of his people that he will grant us an audience." Only Catholics were permitted to sign the petitions and no attempt would be made to coerce anyone into doing so. There were enough blanks for 100,000 names. The documents contained four points:

1. We actively desire Catholic education for the Negro.
2. We feel that it would be more advantageous to the Negro if separate and equal facilities would be provided.
3. We pledge ourselves to actively assist any effort to provide such facilities.
4. If funds are not presently available for providing separate schools, we as a group pledge ourselves wholeheartedly to support the raising of such funds.

In their letter to the Apostolic Delegate, the group made it clear that they did not intend to take any legal action. They noted that they would pledge financial support for adequate educational facilities for blacks, but did not want whites and blacks admitted to the same schools.

On Sunday, October 5, another meeting was held with about 800 attending. A response from the Apostolic Delegate, Archbishop Amleto Cicognani, was read in which he stated that, after the letter of September 20 read in all the churches, "I have nothing to state that could be added to the matter. I am confident that everyone will readily comply with what has been clearly proposed by the ecclesiastical authority of the Archdiocese." The group's leader then asked the people gathered to "please accept a motion that we disband."

He said, "I am...positive there will be no rescinding of the issue. There is only one alternative—to attack the Archbishop and the Catholic faith. I don't intend to jeopardize my religion or that of anyone else." Another spokesperson told the crowd, "The effectiveness of this organization has been destroyed."

A standing vote indicated that more than 90 percent of those attending favored the decision to disband. A prepared statement read: "We have reached an impasse. None of us would scandalize, besmirch or discredit the Catholic

Church. Such action could aid only those who…would destroy Catholicism." With that, resistance to Ritter's decision on desegregation collapsed and the gradual integration of the schools of the archdiocese moved forward.

Support and National Follow-Up

Ritter was not without other moral support in his battle, however. His sister-in-law, Helen Ritter, wrote on September 24, 1947:

> We…wanted you to know that we are thinking of you and with you at this time when your stand on the negro question has aroused such diverse claims to praise and condemnation. Of course, I feel, probably because of Mother's and Daddy's attitudes and training, that yours is the only American position to take, and certainly the only Catholic position. So we congratulate you for going forward on it.

To his friend Thomas D. Sheerin of Indianapolis, Ritter wrote on September 29:

> We are having a great deal of agitation over the negro problem, as you no doubt know. I tried to do quietly and simply what I did in Indianapolis, but over here could not get by the newspaper hounds. They had the information almost overnight and, of course, played it up in the papers. I must say, however, the newspapers in St. Louis have stood by me, and I am being flooded with letters of commendation from all over the country. Perhaps, after all, the release of the publicity is providential and will do the Church some good during these difficult days.

And on October 1, J. Robert Dietz, a student at Catholic University in Washington and graduate of Cathedral High School in Indianapolis, wrote to the archbishop:

> News has reached me by way of the press of your recent valiant action in regard to the racial situation in St. Louis. PRAISE GOD FOR YOUR COURAGE! Would that every prelate throughout the

nation [would] follow your heroic example. Many of my fellow students here are likewise elated by this good news. Our Interracial Council on this campus has as one objective to make other (so-called) Catholic institutions of learning truly Catholic by erasing any racial bar. Your action gives us new inspiration for continued efforts.

Perhaps the strangest note came from Ralph Shaw, state chairman of the Communist Party, who wrote to Ritter saying: "We wish to join with others, Catholic and non-Catholic, in congratulating you for this just stand on a basic democratic issue."

In recognition of his stand, in 1948 Archbishop Ritter was named the winner of the Thomas Jefferson Award by the Council Against Intolerance in America and was honored by the Committee to Abolish Discrimination, a committee of the Congress of Industrial Organizations (CIO). Characteristically, he declined both honors.

Following the Leader

After Ritter integrated the schools, other bishops followed his lead. By May 1954, six border and Southern states had enrolled black students in Catholic schools. Archbishop O'Boyle began the process in the District of Columbia in 1949, followed by Bishop Vincent S. Waters of Raleigh in 1953. Archbishop Lucey in San Antonio acted one month before the U.S. Supreme Court ruled in 1954 in *Brown v. Board of Education* that segregation by color in public schools is a violation of the Fourteenth Amendment to the Constitution. Because of state constitutional prohibitions, public schools in Missouri were not integrated until the *Brown* decision was handed down.

Ritter said later, "I wasn't looking for trouble, but I was ready for it if it developed." Although he made no attempt to consult local civil or legal authorities, he did inquire among his clergy to ascertain the support he might receive from them. "I wanted to know whether they thought it could be done." And it was the widespread assurance of the pastors and curates that it both could and should be done that convinced him to proceed with such a revolutionary step—the first desegregation of any school system, parochial or secular, in any part of the South.

Archbishop Ritter's vision for equality stretched well beyond education and parish boundaries. For example, on April 1, 1954, he wrote the coordinator of Catholic Hospital ministries, Reverend Joseph Winter, M.S.W., at the Catholic Charities Office:

> For some time the thought has come to me that you should give consideration in your hospital work to call a meeting of all the representatives of our Catholic hospitals...for the purpose of laying down a uniform policy in regard to the admission of negroes. There is such a variance among the hospitals now, which is not good. If all would follow the same policy it would be easier for the individual hospitals to make progress along this line. You know how difficult it is and the record of our Catholic hospitals is not good compared to those of interdenominational hospitals.

He followed this up in 1955 in his address to the fortieth annual convention of the Catholic Hospital Association, calling for an end to discrimination in all Catholic hospitals. "Catholic hospitals, along with the whole Church, have a most serious obligation to carry out courageously the teachings of Christ and to put aside their policies and practices and end all discrimination because of race, color, or religion."

By 1963 racial tensions in St. Louis and elsewhere had magnified. The St. Louis Conference on Religion and Race—co-sponsored by Ritter; Rabbi Ephraim Epstein, president of the St. Louis Rabbinical Association; and Dr. W. Sherman Skinner, president of the Metropolitan Church Federation—met for the first time, with a theme of "Challenge to Justice and Love." On Sunday, May 19, the delegates gathered at the Kiel Opera House for a rally, which was followed the next day at the Coronado Hotel by workshops for representatives of the various religious and racial groups. At the close of the conference the Resolutions Committee adopted a statement that read, in part: "We have expressed our own guilt for having contributed to the sin of segregation." It called upon the St. Louis Aldermen to pass a strong and enforceable Fair Housing Law and for the Missouri Legislature to pass, "without any crippling amendments," the Public Accommodations Bill it was then considering.

Through 1963 there were protests and demonstrations over segregated schools, lunch counters, and public swimming pools. On August 11, Ritter sent a letter to be read in all parishes announcing the establishment of an archdiocese Commission on Human Rights. He said that its function would be to "advise and recommend procedures which will bring about a reign of justice and charity in the community; to initiate a program that will enable all to understand the principles involved in the current civil rights issue; and to formulate activities that will overcome the obstacles that now impede the use of God-given rights." Clergy and laity, both black and white, were appointed to the Commission.

Bank Demonstrations

When the Jefferson Bank at 2600 Washington Boulevard, just west of downtown, refused to hire blacks for "white-collar" jobs, the St. Louis branch of the Congress for Racial Equality decided to intervene. Bank officials obtained a court order on August 29, 1963, prohibiting any disruption of business, but not forbidding picketing. So at 4:15 that afternoon, blacks and whites jammed the sidewalks surrounding the bank, singing and marching and filling the bank lobby, where many of the protesters sat on the floor. Mayor Raymond R. Tucker, who had praised the March on Washington led by Dr. Martin Luther King, Jr., held only two days earlier, criticized the local action with its "tactics of disorder."

The day's protest brought the arrest of nine demonstrators, charged with contempt of court for interfering with bank business. After that, CORE (the Congress of Racial Equality) and other groups marched at the bank on an almost daily basis for months, with sixty arrests for violating the judge's order. On October 24, the first nine were sent to the city jail; protesters held rallies and vigils outside, as well as sit-ins at City Hall.

During that summer several companies and labor unions had endorsed a program of equal work opportunity, and that fall hundreds of local businesses, labor unions, and other organizations endorsed a ten-point program developed by the St. Louis Commission on Equal Employment Opportunity. CORE claimed victory and called off its protests in March 1964 after learning that six blacks had been hired for white-collar jobs at the bank.

Institute on Human Rights

On August 28, 1963, Ritter wrote to his priests, announcing a Pastoral Institute on Human Rights to be held at the Park Plaza Hotel in September. "I will preside at all the sessions of this Conference. Every pastor and assistant, be he religious or secular, our teachers as well, are to attend the sessions. I ask that you schedule your calendar so as to be present. We will ask the various clerical houses or religious to take care of sick calls during this time." Among the speakers were Right Reverend George Higgins, director of the Social Action Department of the National Catholic Welfare Conference; Right Reverend Daniel M. Cantwell, chaplain of the Chicago Interracial Council; and Reverend Rollins E. Lambert, assistant director of the Newman Club at the University of Chicago.

During these events, Ritter was also deeply involved in time-consuming preparations for the Second Session of the Vatican Council. It was a measure of his commitment to this cause that he considered the institute important enough to warrant his full participation.

Following the three-day pastoral institute, attended by about 500 priests, Ritter said at a news conference: "Racial injustice is a sin, and it is a serious violation of charity, which is the essence of Christianity. For anyone to go to the altar and receive the Body and Blood of Christ with bitterness in his heart, with hatred in his heart for his fellow man, this certainly would be considered a sacrilege and a great insult to Christ." He then announced that pastors would be establishing seminars for their parishioners patterned on the clergy institute.

Other dioceses became interested in what was happening in St. Louis. Monsignor Joseph L. Bernadin, Vicar General of the Diocese of Charleston, South Carolina, wrote to Monsignor Drumm on October 2, 1963, asking for information on the institute because they were hoping to have a clergy conference on the same subject the following spring.

On November 13, Bishop George J. Gottwald, Chairman of the St. Louis Archdiocesan Commission on Human Rights, sent to each priest in the archdiocese a booklet titled *The Changing Parish*. It contained the thoughts, ideas, and programs recommended by St. Louis priests working in the area of human rights, which they had developed over a series of several meetings among themselves. Two weeks later he sent a letter to the priests promoting a pastoral letter composed by one of the country pastors; prayer cards initially given out at the pastoral institute and now suggested for children in the schools and for use at parish meetings; and *Black Like Me*, a book suitable for parish meetings.

Following the March 25, 1965, civil rights march from Selma to Montgomery, Alabama, Ritter sent a letter to his clergy dated April 1:

> *Once again I call upon the priests of the archdiocese of St. Louis to dedicate themselves wholeheartedly to the struggle for equal rights for all regardless of race. Your response to our initial requests has been in many instances outstanding; much, however, remains to be done. In those parishes where a start has been made in educating our Catholic people about their responsibilities, progress must continue. In those parishes where little or nothing has been done, an honest start must be made. As I reminded the Council of Catholic Men, commitment to the cause of racial justice is imperative for all.*

A National Leader in Education

Archbishop Ritter was a leader in Catholic education, and in 1952 was elected president of the National Catholic Education Association. Among other achievements, he was known as a pioneer in supporting education for children with special needs.

When Father Elmer Behrmann returned from his military chaplaincy, the chancery asked him to pursue a master's degree at Saint Louis University to prepare for assignment as a high school administrator. There he learned that government statistics for 1944 showed an estimated 12.4 percent of children in the United States were classified as "exceptional," of whom 2 percent were mentally retarded. Only about 11 percent of the mentally retarded who required special education were receiving it.

The archdiocese had schools for blind and deaf children, but only St. John the Baptist School in St. Louis had a classroom for children with other disabilities. Father Behrmann decided to dedicate his life to educating mentally retarded children. In June 1950, he placed a notice in the archdiocesan newspaper encouraging parents who had children with special needs to contact him. He received leads to 170 children with mental handicaps. He then visited pastors to obtain classrooms and he was offered space without charge in five parishes. Next he wrote to provincials of all the religious communities staffing schools in the archdiocese. He needed teachers and received three to add to Sister Renata Stoer, the teacher at the St. John the Baptist school.

When Ritter saw the great need and the importance of addressing it, he appointed Behrmann as assistant superintendent for parish schools and director of the Department of Special Education, with the mandate to report directly to Ritter himself. Although some communities of sisters had created schools for exceptional children in the United States in the 1930s and 1940s, St. Louis was the first to provide such education on a diocese-wide basis.

From 1950 to 1980, thirty-one rooms for special education functioned in as many parishes and six special schools were established. In addition, twenty-three programs of catechetical instruction were provided at parishes on Saturday mornings for children not enrolled in the all-day classes. St. Mary's residential school, for children living outside the St. Louis area, was opened for the fall semester in 1952. Over the years other facilities were added, St. Joseph's Vocational Center and two group homes among them. Later, Father Behrmann led a move to request the National Catholic Education Association to establish an office of special education at their headquarters in Washington, D.C., to promote the work in dioceses throughout the country. They did, and he became its first director, spending half of his time at projects in St. Louis and the other half in the nation's capital promoting special education access for all Catholic children in need.

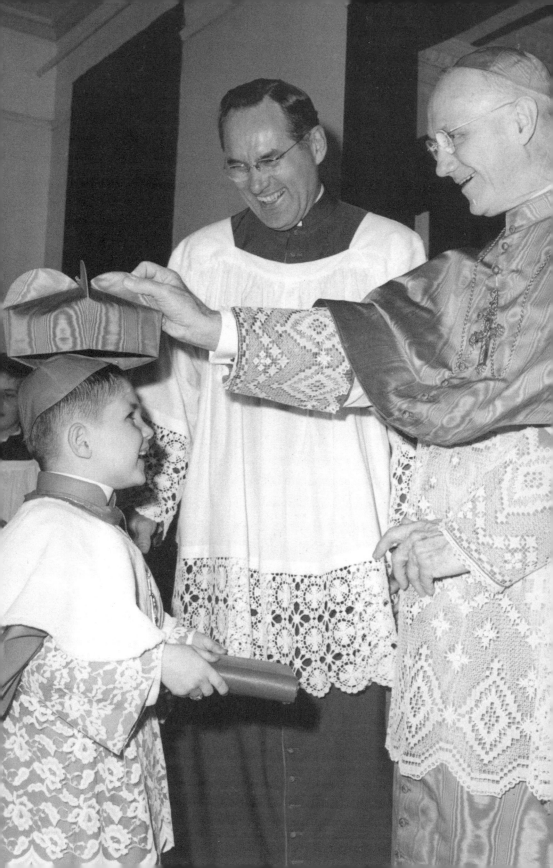

AN ADVOCATE FOR IMMIGRANTS

Among other problems following World War II—though we have already seen that Ritter was given some of the worst, and never shied away—were the waves of immigrants and millions of people displaced by both the war and the Communist takeover of Eastern Europe.

To enhance the Church's response to this great need, Archbishop Ritter sponsored an Institute on Immigration in October 1952, attended by clergy and laypeople concerned with immigration work. In September of that year Ritter had expressed to Archbishop Patrick O'Boyle of Washington, D.C., misgivings about what he considered a "blunder" by the Immigration Department of the National Catholic Welfare Conference. The agency was responsible for making what Ritter thought a poor presentation of the Catholic case regarding the McCarran Act of June 27, 1952, a law that discriminated in favor of northern and western European nations, and contained harsh provisions for eliminating undesirable aliens. Ritter urged that Monsignor John O'Grady of the President's Committee be emboldened to promote the Catholic viewpoint on the immigrant question.

In his talk before the institute, Ritter blasted the McCarran Act, calling it "inconceivable that the people should want to retain in statute such a piece of legislation that is openly and avowedly discriminatory. There is no piece of legislation that the enemies of the United States are using more effectively against us than our recent immigration legislation. The time has come for the American people to disavow this law."

St. Louis was long involved with immigrants through the Central Bureau, originally the Central Verein, established in the 1800s to assist German immigrants moving to the Midwest. By 1956 the local resettlement program had assisted more than 650 families with housing, jobs, and loans. The bureau continued its work into the late 1950s, by then focusing attention on Cuban families. The goal was always to assist displaced people in their struggles to build a new life and become self-supporting citizens.

Archbishop Ritter with Monsignor Elmer Behrmann at St. Mary's Special School.

2

Settling in
St. Louis

SYNODS

Archbishop Ritter presided over two synods in St. Louis, the eighth and ninth in the archdiocese. (A synod is a gathering of bishops, clergy, and laity to discuss issues of importance in a diocese; they are deliberative, not legislative bodies.) Each was a gathering of the clergy to promulgate legislation regarding diocesan activities and affairs, as well as to reinstate diocesan officials in their roles of service. Each synod was preceded by a notice to the clergy inviting them to submit recommendations for inclusion in the archdiocesan statutes so that they might be considered for implementation.

On March 23, 1950, the archbishop sent a letter to all the priests announcing the synod and inviting them to elect one of their number from each deanery to serve on the synodal commission. He also sent a draft—containing 26 pages of legislation with 160 statutes regarding persons, things, and temporal administration—of the proposed synod legislation, and a form for submission of recommendations. The synod took place on May 10 at Kenrick Seminary, with 302 diocesan priests and 52 priests of religious communities participating.

May 10, 1950

Statutes considered at the synod included the following:

+ Statute 18: "In matters of faith and morals, neither priests nor laymen may participate in conferences or discussions with non-Catholics without our approval or that of the Holy See."

+ Statute 82: "There shall be a High Mass each Sunday in every parish."

+ Statute 93: "To foster frequent and daily Holy Communion, we urge the distribution of Communion before and after the Mass on weekdays as well as during the Mass."

+ Statute 103: "We direct that on all Sundays throughout the year there shall be an instruction of at least ten minutes' duration at every Mass in all churches and institutional chapels of the Archdiocese."

Salaries for pastors were set at $1,300 a year; for assistants at $720; and for religious teachers at $450. Besides promulgating the legislation, the archbishop appointed or reappointed the vicar general, chancellor, vice chancellor, assistants to the chancellor, treasurer, secretary, diocesan consultors, matrimonial court personnel, synodal examiners, and synodal judges.

Concern for Priests

Archbishop Ritter was a highly effective leader, and like all such leaders was always concerned for the welfare of his priests. He maintained the practice—first begun in 1874—of providing a yearly retreat for all St. Louis diocesan priests. A provision of the Seventh Diocesan Synod had reaffirmed this practice, and he insisted on its observance. In June each year, two back-to-back retreats were held at Kenrick Seminary, and all active priests were assigned to attend one or the other. Retreat preachers included priests who conducted retreats as their customary occupation, in addition to bishops—Fulton Sheen being the most renowned—and theologians. By 1954 the number of retreatants the Kenrick retreats had grown so large that each year a certain number were directed to make a retreat "at the time and place most convenient to them" (meaning a Kenrick retreat was no longer mandatory, provided they took one somewhere, sometime). The decision to do so was dictated by two concerns: lack of space at Kenrick and a desire to give priests the opportunity every five years to make a retreat on their own.

In 1957 the retreat location was moved to the new seminary facility built by the Passionist Fathers at Warrenton, Missouri, about fifty miles west of St. Louis. That year there were ten retreats—smaller in size—from February to November, and one at Kenrick for the younger men.

By 1960, all of the men went to Warrenton to one of the fifteen yearly retreats. New buildings had been added to the seminary, allowing for more men in each retreat. The Passionist Fathers had also become the normal retreat masters. All diocesan priests were still expected to participate except golden jubilarians, who were encouraged to attend, and priests who were retired. Men of various ages were assigned in the same weeks so they could mingle.

From 1946 until 1964, the Feast of the Sacred Heart was designated as a "Day of Sacerdotal Sanctification." Each priest was encouraged to offer Mass, engage in a private examination of conscience regarding the way he was living his priesthood, make an act of reparation for his sins, spend some time meditating on Jesus as supreme and eternal priest, and observe a holy hour closing with a renewal of personal consecration to the Sacred Heart. In his letter of June 11, 1952, promoting the day, Archbishop Ritter asked each priest to "spend the day in close intimacy with the Sacred Heart," and noted that it was scheduled to occur on "the Friday between the two retreat weeks." Also, beginning in the early 1950s, "Priests' Monthly Days of Recollection" were held at various locations from October through May. The usual hours were from 1:00 to 4:30 PM, and absolute silence was requested. As of 1957, almost 200 men were participating.

retreat houses in St. L. after 1945...

Archbishop Ritter visits with children at the New Cathedral School on Easter Tuesday (April 19), 1960.

PERSONAL WORK ETHIC

Archbishop Ritter, despite his gardening, was a hard worker, perhaps even a workaholic. Between his commitment to his work and the agonizing issues that were presented to him, he had a tendency to overtax himself.

Ritter wrote two letters to Archbishop McNicholas in September 1948—the first (September 9) in response to his friend's concern about his well-being in the aftermath of the desegregation episode of the year before—that reveal some continuing anxiety about his health, as well as his dedication to his work. "It relieved my conscience a great deal to have you say that I should play and relax more. It seems that I don't do much of it and, of course, for that reason I am glad to get the encouragement from you."

Then, on September 22, he wrote: "I am leaving this morning to go far out in the Diocese to take part in the organization of our Catholic Women in the rural areas. It seems that they have been very much neglected." The reference is to the Rural Parish Workers of Christ the King, founded at that time by two women to assist people in need in depressed areas of the archdiocese. The group focused especially on the so-called Lead Belt section southwest of St. Louis, in addition to helping catechize children there who did not attend a Catholic school.

Most Reverend John S. Mix, superior general of the Congregation of the Resurrection, wrote the archbishop concerning his community, and alluded to the second anniversary of Ritter's installation as archbishop of St. Louis, coming on October 7. Ritter replied on October 15: "October 7th passed quietly and, I am glad to say,...happily. Most of the two years were used in getting adjusted to new people and work. However, they have not been too difficult and in the last year I have felt very much at home. Both the people and the Clergy are, indeed, very fine and have shown me every kindness and loyalty." However, the school desegregation issue and the feelings it aroused still hovered as a dark cloud over the diocese; many Catholics persisted in their resistance and their ill will toward the archbishop.

IMPORTANCE OF CURRENT EVENTS

Archbishop Ritter was deeply involved in all of life and did not hesitate to engage in public matters when he thought it necessary. In 1949 he sent a telegram to President Harry Truman: "Deeply concerned about the safety of pilgrims of all faiths to the sacred places of Palestine. We trust that our government will insist on full United Nations sovereignty over Jerusalem and environs as agreed upon in 1947 and 1948 by the United Nations General Assembly. Compromise in this matter will make our country responsible for failure to keep peace in the Near East." Similar telegrams were sent to General Carlos P. Romulo, President of the United Nations General Assembly, and to Mr. Dean Acheson, U.S. Secretary of State. Between 1948 and 1951, 332,000 European Jews moved to Palestine, followed by the creation of the state of Israel in 1952.

Of equal concern to Ritter was keeping his priests abreast of the issues of the day, which was done through annual "Conferences of Priests." The conferences were held four times a year, normally during the Ember Weeks and usually conducted on a deanery basis. Moral cases were always included with other matters. Papers were presented on the subjects assigned, followed by questions to stimulate discussion among the clergy attending. Wide-ranging topics included right-to-work laws, alcohol and drug abuse, religious prejudice, fair wage, and credit unions. Further, there was moral rearmament and Communism, and religious questions regarding revision of rules to further more frequent reception of Communion. By 1963 the presentations had moved to Kenrick Seminary and were given by recognized authorities in their fields.

These conferences were designed to keep the priests well informed so they could effectively serve their people with confidence that they were in touch with current knowledge on matters of importance for their ministry. With the advent of the sixteen documents of Vatican II, a new body of information and thought became accessible and a different system of study and discussion had to be devised so that it could include the laity.

Ember Days/Embertide

As part of the liturgical calendar before the reforms of Vatican II, Ember Days were four sets of three days, all falling within the same week, at the beginning of each of the four seasons. Their purpose, beyond encouraging prayer and fasting, was to thank God for the gifts of nature.

Two Significant Events

Two especially noteworthy religious events happened in St. Louis in 1947. The first happened on April 10, when the archbishop received his pallium in a service at the Cathedral.

Then, on October 26, the archdiocese celebrated its 100th anniversary. When it was formed in 1847, St. Louis had forty-three parishes and seventy-three priests. Ritter used the occasion to consecrate the entire diocese to the Sacred Heart of Jesus and the Immaculate Heart of Mary and to promote the enthronement of the Sacred Heart in every Catholic home. He celebrated a solemn Mass at the Cathedral that Sunday morning, and that evening services of consecration were held in each of the now 307 parishes and missions of the diocese.

In his sermon at the Cathedral Mass, Monsignor Nicholas Brinkman, rector of the Cathedral, said, "Fortunate indeed we are and of inestimable advantage to us is the liberty the Church enjoys under the American constitution. No tyrant here casts chains about her; no concordat limits her actions or cramps her energies. She is free as the eagle upon the Alpine heights."

Day-to-Day Duties

Even in the life of an archbishop, there were always the more-or-less routine, mundane dealings. On November 18, Ritter, who could be caustic if irritated and who resented those who invaded the diocese to obtain money for their own projects elsewhere, wrote to his friend, Archbishop Ryan of Omaha:

> Your professional promoter is again getting in my hair, as you will
> see from the attached clipping. I am wondering whether you would

not again inform him that before coming into the diocese to speak he should have the permission from the Chancery Office. I have nothing against Boy's Town, or Monsignor Flanagan, but I am satisfied that it has long ago become a racket for collecting large sums of money. As you will see, a football game is the occasion of his spending about a week in St. Louis promoting Boy's Town, which long ago ceased to be in need of financial aide [sic].

3

Beginnings

Archbishop Ritter was both a son of Indiana and a former bishop in that state. He had family and friendship ties there. So it is not surprising that in 1948 Ritter had strong bonds to Indianapolis and cared for people in need there. One such couple, having marital problems, wrote to the archbishop to announce that they were divorcing. He responded:

> *With all the earnestness at my command, I would ask you not to go through with this, and to try to effect, if not a reconciliation, at least a truce. You know as well as I do that it would be a terrible breach of a fine tradition of the _____ family and lessen the prestige in which all of you are held in Indianapolis. Another thing—life is short, and why spoil it with something like this? Truly, no real happiness and contentment is going to come to you.*

Historical Perspective

It is no surprise that Ritter maintained ties to Indiana all his life. There he was born, there he grew up, and there he entered the priesthood.

New Albany, Indiana, is in the southeastern corner of the state, across the Ohio River from Louisville, Kentucky. For much of the nineteenth century, New Albany was a riverboat town and home to a thriving boat-building business, which produced the notable *Robert E. Lee* steamboat. Some of the finest homes on Main Street belonged to riverboat captains who made their fortunes transporting goods to merchants in cities and towns up and down the river, and by ferry to Louisville.

When railroads brought a decline in river traffic, the town turned to glass manufacturing as a prime industry. The first plate glass windows manufactured in the United States were installed in the Heib Building in 1870 in New Albany. Later, hardwood and plywood replaced glass production, and today the 37,000 citizens are engaged in many industrial pursuits.

Indiana gained statehood in 1816. Many of the early settlers were Quakers who were opposed to slavery. During the 1820s and 1830s, citizens of Indiana supported the American Colonization Society's efforts to relocate free blacks from the United States to Liberia in Africa. However, few wanted to be deported, so other means of helping had to be devised. By the 1830s a modest number of "Hoosiers" were actively supporting the Underground Railroad in its efforts on behalf of escaped slaves and free blacks. Quakers and members of several Protestant denominations were especially active in this movement.

New Albany was a refuge along the railroad. Second Baptist Church, built between 1849 and 1852 as the Town Clock Church, was a local way station. There still exist small openings to rooms in the dirt-floor basement, left just as they were when fugitive slaves hid in them during their journey north. A plaque in front of the church on Third and Main reads:

A Gateway to Freedom: As early as 1821 enslaved blacks, seeking freedom, crossed the Ohio River from Louisville to New Albany. The antebellum and Civil War periods brought more fugitives. Many freedom-seekers were aided by other slaves and anti-slave whites—all risking violence and arrest. Not everyone who tried succeeded. Many freedom-seekers coming through New Albany achieved their goal, traveling as far north as Canada.

Elmer Joseph Ritter, 1907.

German Family History

During these same years, Germans were immigrating to the United States in large numbers, and many settled in the rich bottomland of the Ohio River Valley. Some—farmers, craftsmen, and shopkeepers from Baden, Bavaria, and Saxony—settled in the vicinity of New Albany. Those who came to Floyd County settled near Falling Run Creek, where they built slaughterhouses, tanneries, and breweries. Tailors, stone carvers, and furniture makers also set up businesses. They often purchased large tracts of land to remain near each other and maintain their cultural identity.

In 1853 the German Catholics in New Albany received permission from Bishop Jacques Maurice de St. Palais of Vincennes to organize a parish and build a church. Five years later, Saint Mary of the Annunciation was dedicated, becoming their spiritual home. It was located just one block from Holy Trinity Parish, established earlier by the Irish Catholics in the town.

Among the German immigrants were the Ritter family from Koblenz and the Luettes, part French, from Alsace-Lorraine. The patriarch of the Ritters was a farmer, his son a stonemason who helped build one of the first bridges across the Ohio River. Nicholas Ritter, born in May 1857, belonged to the third generation and learned the baker's trade. When he was seventeen, he opened his own business in New Albany at the corner of East Oak and 13th Street. He married Bertha Luette, who had been born in October 1865, and they were blessed with six children: Henry, Edmund, Frank, Elmer Joseph, Carl, and Catherine. The family lived above the store, and the baking was done in a separate building behind. The Ritters remained there for two generations, enjoying enough success to provide a satisfactory education for the children.

Family photo from 1936, Louisville, Kentucky. Joseph Elmer is on the left in the middle row, seated next to his mother and father.

Elmer Joseph Ritter, the fourth child, was born on July 20, 1892, and baptized six days later at Saint Mary's. His godparents were Joseph Luette and Anna Mechler and the presiding priest was the pastor, Reverend Edward J. Faller. Elmer attended Saint Mary's school and when old enough took his turn serving Mass.

One of his boyhood friends, Julius Moser, later recalled the speeches Elmer delivered from the landing near the stained-glass window inside the Ritter home while pretending to offer Mass. Another friend, Herman Emglinger, son of a New Albany butcher, remembered how they practiced the same ritual, with Elmer usually taking the role of the priest. Later he said that his desire to be a priest was due, in part, "to a religious and saintly grandmother who went to church every morning." In an interview toward the end of his life, Elmer recalled:

> As long as I can remember I wanted to be a priest. As a little fellow going to school, I recall the first few days that I was at school and the children were going to confession. It was for the Ember Days. Of course, I wasn't prepared to go to confession, but I wanted to go. And the nun told me, she said: "Maybe some day you will hear confessions… You will be a priest." I think that nun solidified me in my desire to be a priest.

An uncle, Dr. Harry N. Ritter, influenced three of the Ritter boys to enter the medical profession. Henry became an eye specialist, Edmund a dentist, Frank a surgeon. After their father died, Carl ran the bakery until he went into the insurance business. The one daughter, Catherine, remained at home to care for her mother until she died, after which Catherine became a nun. Later, the priest-son said of his father, "He saw that we all had a broad education and all the opportunities. We had horses, a surrey, sleighs in the winter, bicycles, all the things children could want, and yet we weren't rich. Father lived to be 87. When I was made a bishop he sent me a $1,000 check with a note that this was coming to me because my education had not been as expensive as my brothers'."

As they grew up, all the brothers worked at the bakery. The boys at school gave him the nickname "Apple-Pie Elmer."

Elmer and his friend Herman decided in seventh grade to go to the seminary. They told the assistant, Father Borries, who suggested that they make arrangements to enter St. Meinrad Archabbey (Seminary; in St. Meinrad, Indiana) after they finished eighth grade. Elmer received parental consent immediately; Herman's parents told him to finish high school first. In the first year of college they were reunited.

SEMINARY YEARS

Elmer entered St. Meinrad Seminary as a boarding student at the age of fourteen on September 12, 1906. In 1910, he moved to the junior college level, and he began theology studies in 1913. In the St. Louis archives are twenty-one notebooks from his seminary days with extremely detailed synopses of dogma (eleven notebooks), morals, liturgy, patristics, and Scripture. The cover of each is signed "E. J. Ritter"; the final one, dated 4/17/17 and devoted to "De Sacrificio Missae" has "Elmer J. Ritter."

The notebooks are carefully written in close thought patterns, and reveal an exceptionally ordered mind. Written for the most part in impeccable Latin, they suggest a solid command of that language. There are also occasional passages in English, often as a further commentary on a passage quoted or developed.

These notebooks are a treasure trove of information on the way theology was taught and received in the early decades of the twentieth century. Very scholastic in content and style, the notes manifest a mind that was logical, careful about details, diagrammatic in thought, and thoroughly inclusive.

Analyzing their contents is fascinating. The handwriting is very clear and consistent, the entries carefully composed, implying that they would be the subject of further study outside the classroom. There are no references to textbooks; perhaps none were used. The pages are tightly but neatly arranged, with one thesis after another in logical order. They have the marks of having been formulated by a scholar who was serious about his studies and both eager to learn and to retain for life what he learned.

Philosophy II class, 1912, at St. Meinrad Seminary. In the front row are Leo DuFraine, Norbert Spitzmesser, O.S.B., Paul Thoma, O.S.B., Sylvester Eiseman, O.S.B., and Elmer J. Ritter. Standing behind them are Carl Riebenthaler, John Dapp, James Maloney, Clement Bosler, Joseph Newman, Otto Peters, Frederio Rothermal, and Aloysius J. Copenolle.

The notebooks also reflect the theological process as practiced in the seminaries of that day. Professors lectured and students recorded the contents of the lectures for private study. There was little place for individual or personal reflection. The learning process was rather a repetition of what the teacher had said so that it could be given back either in succeeding class questioning or during tests and examinations.

Ritter's remarks in English offer interesting insights. On the Gospel of Matthew, Elmer noted:

> The Gospel of the Lord according to St. Matthew is not arranged chronologically but topologically—arranged in topics. We must remember that there is a difference between historian and evangelist. The former only relates facts as they are, but the latter picks out certain topics which will prove what he intends to prove. It is to be deplored that they did not write more in chronological order for then we would perhaps have a better, more extensive knowledge of the life of Christ. However this is only speaking from a human standpoint. Almighty God willed it to be as it is & hence it is best to be satisfied with what we have. The writings of the Evangelist are rather memoirs than history.

The notes also include an interesting view from a time period when a strictly literal interpretation of the Scripture was mandatory.

Elmer noted this on atheism:

> "Practical—He who acts as though there were no God—many; heretical—He who denies there is a God—(Ingersoll), Rousseau, Voltaire; positive—He who directly denies the existence of God— those who know scientifically there is no God; negative—who simply know nothing of God. Can there be an ignorantia Dei?—There is no invincible ignorance.

Or this on the Assumption of Mary:

> *The Assumptio BVM is ripe for definition—Census Communis—*
> *Theological reasons—not derogatory to Xt whose body & soul into*
> *heaven before general day of Resurrection; the flesh that furnished*
> *humanity to Xt could not have suffered corruption; Ex Immacul.*
> *Concept.*

Thirty-five years later, Pope Pius XII declared this an article of faith, thus offering a ray of hope to a world still suffering from the nightmarish aftermath of widespread war.

It is evident that the notebooks were valued possessions, as Elmer kept them all his life. In one there are two sheets of letterhead stationery imprinted: "Bishop's House, 1347 Meridian St., Indianapolis, Ind." They contain summary items in Latin and English of points he planned to make in two talks. They are not dated but show the same care and logical development as do the seminary notebooks.

Ritter hoped that, after his ordination, he would be sent to Rome for further study. Had that happened, there is no doubt he would have become a successful dogma professor. But in the winter of 1917, Germany announced the resumption of its unrestricted U-boat campaign, and on February 26 President Wilson asked Congress for permission to arm American merchant ships. The United States was moving closer to declaring war, which effectively ended Atlantic travel except for extreme emergency or troop transport needs. It also ended Elmer's dream of theological study in Rome.

Lifelong Devotion
to His Educational Roots

Not surprisingly, Ritter retained a deep lifelong regard for St. Meinrad. In October 1954, he sent an article titled "The Bishop and His Priests," which he had written at the request of the seminary and which was very well received. The request, from Reverend Adrian Fuerst, O.S.B., quoted Father Frowin Conrad as saying, "We can't go to press without our Number One Alumnus!"

On January 31, 1956, Ritter wrote to Right Reverend Bonaventure Knaebel, coadjutor abbot, to thank him for the gift he had brought on a visit to St. Louis. "How lovely is the statue of Our Lady of Einsiedeln. I am planning to give it a place of prominence in my study. It will be a remembrance and souvenir of the happy occasion of your Abbatial blessing." He had preached on that occasion at the abbot's invitation and had said, in part:

> St. Meinrad's is our Monte Casino, a watchtower of Christianity, a Christian lighthouse, the Mount Sinai of monasticism in Indiana and the Middle West. May it ever remain like its prototype—beyond destruction, preserving for us all the powerful breath of life and piety which St. Benedict of Nursia bequeathed to his followers, and silently but forcefully proclaiming its motto, Ora et labora as the path to holiness to all men.

Later in a letter to Very Reverend Anselm Schaaf, O.S.B., Westminster Abbey, Mission City, B.C., Canada, he wrote: "Word came to me last week of the death of dear Father Benedict at Marmion. I could not go to the funeral as we were burying one of our Provincials here on the same day. I will always treasure his memory along with the holy monks who guided my faltering steps."

In 1958, as he made plans to celebrate his twenty-fifth anniversary as a bishop, Elmer asked how many men he had ordained while bishop of Indianapolis. The reply indicated that, from 1934 to 1946, "Your Excellency ordained 210 young men to the Priesthood at St. Meinrad."

ORDINATION AND
EARLY PASTORAL ASSIGNMENTS

Elmer Joseph Ritter was ordained at St. Meinrad on May 30, 1917, by Bishop Joseph Chartrand of Indianapolis. The archives of that diocese contain the parchments regarding both his final grade as a student—it was 99½ percent and he received the degree "Summa Cum Laude," and the document attesting to his ordination to the priesthood. They both contain the word "Vladimirium" for his first name, someone having decided it as the appropriate Latin equivalent of Elmer. He was also listed in the Academic Report for that year as "Prefect of the Seminary," a role he served in his diaconate year.

Father Ritter celebrated his first Mass at Saint Mary of the Annunciation, his home parish, on Sunday, May 31, 1917, followed a few days later by witnessing the marriage of his brother Frank to Lula May Kraft on June 4.

On July 7 he was assigned to St. Patrick Church in Indianapolis. A personal note from Bishop Chartrand accompanied the letter of assignment, indicating that the appointment was temporary. The bishop knew of Ritter's desire to study in Rome and perhaps was offering that possibility for the near future. On October 12, Father Ritter received a second letter of appointment, this time to Saints Peter and Paul Cathedral as assistant to the rector, who was the bishop himself.

Since Ritter and Chartrand lived together in the Cathedral rectory, the bishop could observe firsthand the activities of his young assistant and became dependent on him to the point that he decided he could not spare him. So on May 20, 1924, Father Ritter received word that Pope Pius XI had conferred on him the honorary degree of Doctor of Sacred Theology, which meant that he would not leave Indianapolis to study abroad. The bishop, who had secured the degree, was no doubt pleased. His assistant's feelings about the matter were not recorded.

Just over a year later, on August 25, 1925, Bishop Chartrand appointed Father Ritter, then age thirty-three, to succeed him as rector of the Cathedral. Interestingly, in the original letter assigning him as assistant, he was addressed as "Elmer J. Ritter," but the letter appointing him as rector referred to "Joseph E. Ritter" and it is signed not only by the bishop, but also by Reverend Joseph E. Hamill, assistant to the chancellor. The name change seemed intentional, although Father Ritter continued to use his given name on official documents such as baptismal records.

In due time the new rector also was appointed a diocesan consultor, a member of the diocesan council on administration and finance, and was instrumental in raising funds to build Cathedral High School. Later he became vicar general and served as vice president of *The Indiana Catholic and Record*, the official diocesan newspaper, which eventually became *The Criterion*.

Chartrand, an early advocate of frequent Communion as promoted by Pope Pius X in his decree of July 26, 1906, was known as the "Bishop of the Eucharist." A saintly man and a tower of strength and fervor where religious matters were concerned, the bishop lacked abilities needed for business administration and financial matters. Father Ritter offered him powerful support through difficult times.

The Ku Klux Klan, a great power in Indiana of the mid-1920s, was hostile toward the Catholic Church. Further, the Depression had a devastating impact on both the Church and the general community. In this difficult situation and with failing health, Chartrand recognized that he was no longer up to the task of leading the diocese. In 1933, he petitioned Rome for an auxiliary bishop and recommended Father Ritter.

Installation as Auxiliary Bishop

Rome agreed with Bishop Chartrand's recommendation, and Ritter was elected to the titular see of Hippo and appointed auxiliary bishop of Indianapolis on February 3, 1933. Sometime during this period, he changed his name and became known as Joseph Elmer Ritter, the name under which he was consecrated a bishop by Bishop Chartrand on March 28, 1933.

Terminology

See

A *see* is an archbishop's or bishop's jurisdiction. The see city of a diocese or archdiocese is the community in which the bishop resides and has his cathedral.

Holy See

This term is from the Latin *sancta sedes* (holy chair). The term is derived from the enthronement ceremony of the bishops of Rome (but the "chair" does not refer to the actual chair of Peter and the pontiffs). The Holy See is the universal government of the Catholic Church and operates from the Vatican City State.

Titular see

A *titular see* is a diocese (or archdiocese) that now exists in title only. It is led by a titular bishop or archbishop, a bishop who is not a diocesan ordinary but either an official of the Holy See, an auxiliary bishop, or the head of a jurisdiction that is equivalent to a diocese.

Bishop Ritter in Indianapolis in 1933.

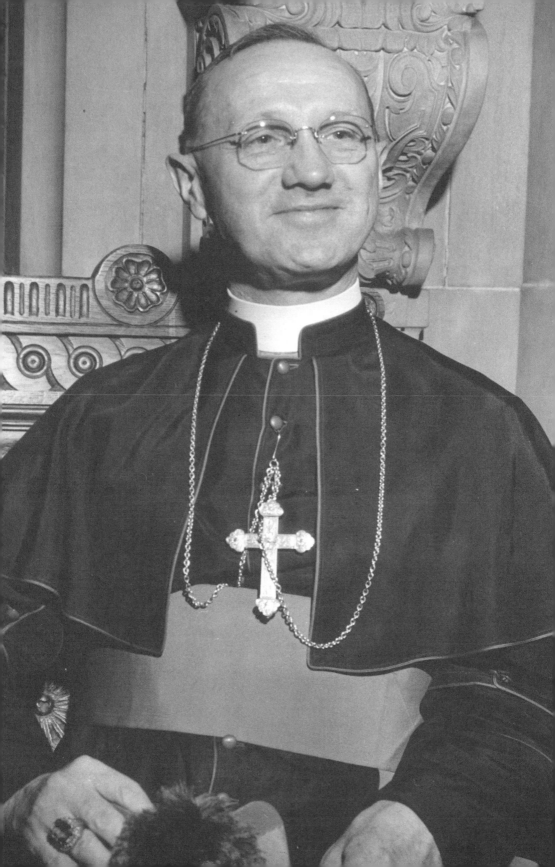

Years later, Ritter noted that his consecration as bishop occurred during the Depression. "As an indication of how bad things were [financially], the banquet that followed my consecration cost just $1.25 a plate, and that included music." His parents—living in Louisville at the time—and siblings attended the ceremony. That same year his home parish of Saint Mary's was celebrating its diamond jubilee and produced a book commemorating the event, which said of the new bishop: "With his winning personality, a charming appearance, keen mind, close application, and willingness at all times to be a producer, his bishop did not make a mistake in beginning immediately the holy work of training him for the Episcopacy. As a boy he led, as a Priest in Indianapolis he was a leader, and as a Bishop he will continue to lead."

On December 8, 1933, Bishop Chartrand died of a heart attack at the Cathedral rectory after receiving the last sacraments from Bishop Ritter. He was sixty-three years old when he died.

INSTALLATION AS BISHOP OF INDIANAPOLIS

Bishop Joseph E. Ritter was installed as Bishop of Indianapolis by the metropolitan, Archbishop McNicholas, on March 24, 1934, making him the youngest ordinary in the American hierarchy. In his sermon that day he observed that he was the first Indiana-born priest to serve as a bishop in the state. He also paid tribute to his predecessors, especially Bishop Chartrand:

> It was our privilege and joy to be intimately associated with him for many years, and the memory of his life and example will always be our inspiration. And as he looks down upon us this morning, we assure him that his work of intensifying the spiritual life of the diocese will go on, not simply because it is his, but because it is the work of Christ and because it is really the solution of all the problems of society.

ACCOMPLISHMENTS IN INDIANAPOLIS

In an interview at the time, the new bishop listed his three goals: "(1) to live in the shadow of a significant predecessor; (2) to maintain the intense devotion instilled by Bishop Chartrand; and (3) to put diocesan finances back in good shape." To accomplish the third, Ritter sought advice from lay experts in the fields of business—bankers, lawyers, and businessmen—and took the steps necessary to "bolster, rehabilitate, and build."

An article in *The Indiana Catholic and Record* of March 30, 1934, commented:

> *Ritter comes to his new office with many of the qualities of all his predecessors. He is possessed of the deep piety of the saintly Bruté, the firmness of de la Hailandière, the kindness and consideration of De Saint Palais, the scholarship of Bishop Chatard, and the qualities of Bishop Chartrand, in whose school he was trained…Young in years, [Ritter] is gifted with a reserve that might well be the adornment of men many years his senior.*

Fiduciary Responsibility

Bishop Ritter took up his new responsibilities with energy and determination. Despite the Depression, between 1934 and 1944 he reduced the diocesan debt by more than three million dollars. To accomplish this feat, he appointed an advisory board and on December 5, 1934, he sent a letter to all pastors regarding financial matters. He wrote:

> *We cannot entertain any thought of a reduction of the present money requirements for the Diocese, as our report clearly shows. The manner of collecting these moneys, however, will be changed, on our part, beginning February 1, 1935. By that time, we direct that all 1934 assessments be paid in full, and that your annual report be sent, in duplicate, to the Chancery. Accompanying your report we require that you enclose a copy of the printed financial report we directed you to make and distribute to your parishes and missions, in our letter of last July.*

Ritter had determined that strong action was needed to overcome their financial problems. He was ahead of his time in prescribing that each pastor provide a detailed financial report for parishioners.

In a time of financial stress, with many potential pitfalls, the bishop was concerned that parish money was being invested without his approval.

On June 18, 1935, he wrote to his priests: "I am writing to warn you against making any investments of parish funds without my advice and permission…If your present investments are convertible place the money with the Diocese, or if the parish has a debt pay off the debt. This note is going out to all parishes that have funds on hand, because solicitors of questionable securities are about."

Another letter to his priests, dated January 8, 1936, noted that the 1935 diocesan indebtedness was reduced by $33,885.78, leaving a debt of $776,403.44 plus the seminary balance of $36,600.00. Listing the figures to the exact penny rather than rounding them was an attempt by the bishop to impress Catholics of the diocese with the care he took in his stewardship over diocesan funds.

After he became the ordinary of the diocese, Bishop Ritter wanted to move from the Cathedral rectory. As he explained it in a letter: "I have been living at the Cathedral Rectory and my position is often embarrassing, to put it mildly. Bishop Chartrand lived in the Cathedral Rectory all of his life, but he was also the Cathedral pastor. I am not, and in my judgment should not try to be pastor of a church and at the same time Bishop of a Diocese." He wrote to two benefactors that he had found a "modest home just outside the city, and the price was $18,600." He asked them to each provide half the cost, which they did.

After the successful appeal, he was able to send his priests a letter telling them of his plan to move. "The new residence is located in the northwest section of Marion County, on what is called Spring Mill Road. The house has seven rooms and the grounds comprise three and a half acres, mostly hillside…It will be necessary to spend $4,000 or $5,000 on the place, which includes building a garage and quarters for the help." Moving allowed him to have a garden, which, with walking and an occasional round of golf, provided his principal recreations.

Nuts-and-Bolts Involvement

Consistent with his understanding of the importance of education that was evident in so many ways throughout his life, Bishop Ritter was concerned with both the state of public instruction and the news media. He worried that the people of the diocese were not receiving solid teaching and news. Therefore, he promoted the diocesan newspaper with a February 1938 pastoral letter in which he decried

> ...the logical consequence of the irreligious education that has prevailed in America during the past hundred years. In a society which neither knows nor fears God, the pestilence of immoral literature takes a heavy toll. To counteract the effects of this poisonous atmosphere we need a powerful antidote. A strong, vigorous Catholic press, providing true, wholesome, Christian thought can supply this need.

While urging all Catholics of the diocese to subscribe to the paper so that they might be solidly informed, the bishop was equally concerned about the quality of diocesan preaching, and sent out sermon outlines for Sundays and special seasons such as Lent. This practice continued into the 1940s.

COMMITMENT TO CATHOLIC EDUCATION

Bishop Ritter carried a deep conviction of the importance of education. This showed itself over and again in Indiana (and later in St. Louis), appearing in the emphasis on the diocesan Catholic newspaper and, later, on using the new medium of television to the benefit of the Church. This conviction was especially strong as it pertained to Catholic elementary and secondary—and even postsecondary—education.

On August 28, 1941, he sent a letter concerning the obligation of parents to send their children to the Catholic school, instructing that it be read at all Sunday Masses. He quoted the Code of Canon Law and added, "In addition to this general legislation and to emphasize the seriousness of the responsibility of parents in this regard, the Bishops of the ecclesiastical province ordained that parents who refuse to send their children to Catholic schools when they are available are to be denied the Sacraments, and absolution from sin is reserved to the Bishop of the Diocese." Pretty strong stuff.

Then in a July 31, 1943, letter on the same subject, he toned down his earlier message a bit, but still held, "When schools, high schools and colleges are available, and when financial reasons do not exist, parents most emphatically sin, and sin grievously, in failing to provide for the religious and moral training of their children as prescribed by the laws of the Church."

One hindrance for the people, however, was that, though money became more plentiful in the 1940s as the war effort expanded and jobs became more readily available, debts incurred during the Depression still made it difficult for parents to pay for Catholic education while meeting the tax burden of support to the public school system. Many were unable to pay for education at religious schools when they could send their children to public schools without cost.

THE WAR YEARS

Catholic Participation in the War Effort

It was for good reason World War II was called a "world" war: it affected everyone. Along with the many new jobs from the expanded industrial support for the war effort, which helped the recovery from the Depression, there was also major disruption as men were called to military service and women entered the workforce. The Church was not exempt from the turbulence, and by 1943 twenty-free priests from Ritter's diocese were serving as U.S. Army or Navy chaplains.

On December 31, 1941, Ritter sent a letter to his priests regarding Civil Defense committees being formed in every town and city. He urged that a priest or Catholic representative be a member of such committees, and that each should form a committee within his own parish.

A wartime concession by Pope Pius XII allowed bishops "to permit the faithful of their dioceses who are engaged in works of National Defense and must work after midnight, to receive Holy Communion without observing the prescribed fast." The concession was given "for the duration of the war."

Among the many shortages impacting the nation—a result of the need to supply military forces engaged in the fighting—was a scarcity of automobile tires. The Church was, of course, was no stranger to this problem, and on May 9, 1942, Bishop Ritter sent this short letter to his priests:

The tire situation is most acute. No priest should ask for new tires unless absolutely necessary for pastoral works. Pastors of rural churches and with missions need automobiles for their work, but most of the priests in cities and towns can dispense with them. Where there is more than one priest at a parish and more than one car, no application should be made to the Tire Rationing Boards until all the tires of all the cars have been used up. One car for parish use is sufficient even though there is more than one priest assigned to that parish. This is a very small contribution we can make to our country and towards winning the war. We will make it cheerfully and generously.

Circumstances compelled cooperation, but the extent of the cheerfulness and generosity is certainly a matter for conjecture.

Evangelism and Financial Development

In September 1938, Ritter inaugurated the first "motor missions" to non-Catholics. Two priests were assigned to this apostolate and given a parish in a rural area of the diocese. This street-preaching missionary movement was directed toward the "separated brethren" in the southern half of Indiana. Ritter requested each Catholic family to set aside two dollars from their Lenten sacrifices to fund the motor mission work in a time of tight finances.

Bishop Ritter believed in growth, in bringing increasing numbers into the church. Despite his determination, however, because of the Depression and World War II only three new parishes were founded during his time in Indianapolis: Saint Christopher, Christ the King, and Saint Thomas Aquinas. He did, however, complete the construction of the impressive entrance to the Cathedral. Work on that project had started under his direction after Easter 1936 and was finished by that Christmas.

One of his Indianapolis confidants was Thomas D. Sheerin, who owned an investment company. In a memo to Ritter dated March 6, 1941, Sheerin noted, "Church finance is emphatically not the same as secular and no layman is fitted to deal with it until he has had time to get his bearings and appraise the essential differences." He went on to say, "The diocese is in excellent credit and has an immediately available line of credit of $300,000.00 at one of the local banks which could be considerably expanded if occasion arose." He closed by supporting the retention of practices then in place, including the following:

+ A report to pastors of the diocesan finances at the end of the year
+ An annual report by each pastor of the "full income, expense and condition" of his parish
+ An up-to-date accounting system for the chancery
+ Full and immediate remittance of all diocesan collections
+ Maintaining monthly installment payments of diocesan assessments
+ Encouraging the use of a standard parish accounting system

In the fall of 1943, Bishop Ritter held a clergy conference on economic issues. He presented a report showing that loans from the reserve funds of the various parishes amounted to $540,331.91 and that the diocesan debt had been reduced from $491,000 to $443,861.73 (12 percent), not a significant amount considering the increase in earning power that the war had generated. After the report, the remainder of the day was devoted to presentations on Pope Pius XI's encyclical On Reconstruction of the Social Order (*Quadragesimo Anno*) and economic life, the Wage and Hour law, the significance of Social Security, and legislation and Catholic action. Holding such a discussion day while the country was at war was evidence of his commitment to the involvement of his diocese in the affairs of the country as well as the affairs of the Church.

Installation of Joseph Ritter as the first archbishop of Indianapolis, December 19, 1944.

A New Archdiocese, A New Archbishop

Pope Pius XII, in December 1944, designated Indiana as a Catholic Province and Indianapolis became an Archdiocese. Until then the state had been part of the Cincinnati Province. With the change, Bishop Ritter became the first archbishop of Indianapolis, making him also, at age fifty-two, the youngest archbishop in the United States. Two new dioceses were created for the state—Evansville and Lafayette—which, together with Indianapolis and Fort Wayne, brought the number to four. Archbishop Ritter was installed at the Cathedral by the Apostolic Delegate, Archbishop Amleto Cicognani, on December 19. The day before there was a reception at the Cathedral High School auditorium during which the new archbishop gave a brief history of the Church in Indiana and paid tribute to Bishop Chartrand, saying it was Chartrand who made the occasion possible.

Thomas Sheerin also spoke, saying that the general public knew the new archbishop as a competent administrator, but his own people knew of his regard for the separated brethren, his generous solicitude "for the unfortunate, his zeal for a wider and deeper education of the laity, his untiring efforts to have the Gospel preached in all the beauty and purity of its divine message."

Archbishop Ritter in Indianapolis in 1944.

In early 1945 Archbishop Ritter took part in two significant episcopal events: the installation of Bishop Henry J. Grimmelsman of Evansville on January 3 and the consecration of Bishop John G. Bennett of Lafayette on January 10. At the dinner following the installation of Bishop Grimmelsman, Ritter paid tribute to Pope Pius XII:

> *The world today is looking to the Papacy as a spiritual power that may be able to affect some semblance of unity, whose influence may still be strong enough to bring order into a chaotic world and prescribe the remedies to heal the wounds of society...In Rome in 1939 I recalled the visit of the Holy Father to our country when he was Papal Secretary of State and he told me that his visit to the United States was the greatest experience of his whole life. At that time the clouds of war were gathering and he said: "Bishop, it will be awful, it will engulf the whole world."*

A week later, preaching at the consecration of Bishop Bennett, he focused on the role of the bishop:

> *There is a relationship of interdependence between the Bishop and the faithful of his diocese. They are his own, and he belongs to them. They belong to each other and have mutual rights in one another. The Bishop must lead, he must teach and he must rule. He must spend himself on behalf of his people. The people must follow him if they are to know and have eternal life.*

With these words Ritter was voicing his own convictions about the bishop and his role in the Church. As time would make abundantly plain, he lived this vision in his own life in an exceptional way, becoming a model for other bishops of the United States who willingly acknowledged the leadership he provided for them.

A New Assignment

On February 22, 1946, Pope Pius XII sent Archbishop Ritter his sacred pallium, the hallowed symbol of his office as archbishop and metropolitan of the Indiana Province. Seemingly, Archbishop Ritter was now set for life as spiritual leader for the Catholic faithful who were placed under his care.

One of Ritter's friends, Elmer A. Steffen, had a summer retreat on Lake Maxinkuckee near Culver, Indiana. Ritter would go there whenever the occasion presented itself, especially in July, a month of high temperatures and reduced activity. Returning home on Sunday, July 21, he stopped at the chancery office and checked his private mail.

The top letter had the seal of the Apostolic Delegation in Washington, D.C. Dated July 20, his birthday, the letter announced that Pius XII had selected him, subject to his acceptance, to succeed the late John Cardinal Glennon of St. Louis. It was the second time he was asked to replace a seemingly irreplaceable man. He accepted, and the appointment was announced by the Apostolic Delegate on Friday, July 26, the anniversary of his baptism. The St. Louis Archdiocese was one of the most historic in the United States. From that moment on, Archbishop Ritter's attention centered primarily on St. Louis.

Farewell to Indianapolis

Archbishop Ritter wrote his last pastoral letter—a letter of farewell—to the Catholics of Indianapolis on August 30, 1946: "In taking my leave of you I assure you that I carry with me pleasant memories of a happy relationship, both official and personal, with the clergy, religious and laity during the years of my administration of the Diocese. With Saint Paul I can say in truth 'you have been my joy and my crown.'"

Family was important for Ritter, and he always tried to be present for holiday dinners, either at the family home in New Albany or in Louisville after his parents moved there. He gave his ten nieces and nephews their first Communion prayer books, rosaries, and scapulars. Helen Ritter, his niece, described him as a "kind, thoughtful man with extremely good taste in his relations with other people." She attributed this to his mother's influence and noted that his father was "a very shrewd business man" who provided an education for all of his children "with the proceeds of a nickel-and-dime bakery." He celebrated many family sacramental events, including the funerals of his mother, who died on December 13, 1941, and his father, whose death occurred on June 6, 1943. Leaving Indianapolis meant leaving his family.

On October 6, 1946, Archbishop Ritter was celebrant at the closing of Forty Hours devotion at the Cathedral. That evening a reception was held at Marian College at which he was given a Chrysler car and a gift of money from the archdiocese, as well as a handsome clock from the clergy. On his departure, an Indiana banker said the archbishop had one of the best business minds in the state, and the diocesan paper noted that he would be remembered "for his Herculean efforts to relieve the diocese of severe indebtedness, incurred from school construction in the 1920s."

Forty Hours Devotion

Forty Hours Devotion is a devotion in which continuous prayer is made for forty hours before the exposed Blessed Sacrament. The focus of the devotion is on the Holy Eucharist. The devotion is named in honor of the forty hours during which the body of Christ is considered to have rested in the tomb.

The next day he boarded a special car on the New York Central railroad and began his farewell trip across Indiana to his destination, the city his predecessor, Cardinal Glennon, described as "The Rome of the West."

4

St. Louis
The Middle Years

CARDINAL GLENNON CHILDREN'S HOSPITAL

One of the unfulfilled dreams of John Cardinal Glennon, Archbishop Ritter's predecessor, was to build a hospital for children. A fundraising brochure promoting the project would state: "There was a cherished dream that centered in children—children of all races and creeds—who were always the special objects of his affection. For them he would build a refuge against pain and sickness and the ravages of disease; for them, a hospital of their own to heal and comfort; and, for St. Louis, added prestige as an outstanding medical center of the nation."

Doctor Peter G. Danis vowed to fulfill the cardinal's dream and sought Ritter's support. On August 21, 1949, the archbishop sent a letter to all parishes announcing a memorial to John J. Cardinal Glennon in the form of a hospital for children. The project would cost $5,000,000.00 and would be called the Cardinal Glennon Memorial Hospital for Children.

A fundraising committee was appointed, composed of representatives of both the diocese and the community. A campaign was developed with special emphasis on the parishes. Meetings were held for deans, for deanery chairmen, for parish chairmen, and for chairmen with their parish teams. Pledge cards were distributed with final instructions on May 9, 1950. The kickoff for solicitations began on May 14 with the final returns due on May 23.

By June 1 the first phase of the campaign was completed, and $4,701,600.00 had been generated in pledges, 94 percent of the goal. In September, Ritter hosted a dinner of thanks for key members of the campaign committee.

Recognizing that prayer was a powerful ingredient in such a project, he turned for aid to the Vatican. On January 29, 1950, he wrote to Monsignor Alfredo Ottaviani, of the Holy Office, asking for prayer and alerting the Holy See that the enterprise was under consideration:

> *At the present time we are making elaborate plans for a great campaign to raise funds for a Children's Hospital in Saint Louis, as a memorial to the late Cardinal Archbishop. I ask a little remembrance in your good prayers for its success. There is no such hospital in the whole United States under Catholic management and we hope that Saint Louis will be the first to have one.*

It was soon clear that additional effort was needed: A pledge is not cash, and cash was necessary for construction. People needed encouragement to honor their pledges. In 1952 Ritter made that the primary practice for Lent in his annual Lenten letter. During December 1952 he interviewed each pastor of the city and county relative to the campaign, since 1953 would be the last year for the payment of pledges. Because there was not time to do the same for all outstate parishes, on February 2, 1953, he sent a letter of encouragement to those pastors, saying, "I am depending on a 100% payment by each parish so that we can make the Cardinal Glennon memorial a successful reality."

During the four-year campaign, some 100,000 St. Louis residents gave $7,000,000 for the project. By the time the contracts were let, the six-story medical center's cost had risen to approximately $5,897,000. A nationally recognized hospital consultant—Neergaard, Agnew and Craig—was brought in to survey the area in order to promote interest in the hospital within the wider civic community. Their report pointed out that, despite a startling increase in the number of births, "there has been little…increase in the number of hospital beds for children in…St. Louis since 1930. A children's hospital is definitely needed." Of 3,973 physicians registered in Missouri in 1949, only seventy-five were pediatricians. Research in children's diseases was not keeping pace with other fields of medicine. Outpatient departments of St. Louis hospitals were pitifully overcrowded. There were no centers for care of premature babies in the city. There was a drastic shortage of beds for convalescent care of long-term cases, and the infant mortality rate in St. Louis was the highest of any large city in the country.

In announcing the groundbreaking, Archbishop Ritter said, "We are grateful to the thousands of people who have sacrificed so much in time and in money to make this great medical institution a reality. The completed hospital will not only be a fitting memorial to my revered predecessor, but a monument to the generosity and devotion of the people of our entire area."

In March 1955, he wrote to John Cardinal D'Alton, Archbishop of Armagh, Ireland, inviting him to dedicate the hospital sometime in November of that same year. D'Alton answered that he had schedule conflicts and could not come. On April 12, Ritter wrote D'Alton again, telling him that the building construction would not be finished until the spring of 1956 and asked him to come then, telling him "there would be no other obligations placed upon you by us than the dedication itself, which would involve a Pontifical High Mass by Your Eminence in our Cathedral on the morning of the dedication and one address at the formal banquet...the evening of that same day."

In a later letter, Ritter specified April 15, 1956, as the date for the dedication. The archbishop was keen on having D'Alton because he had been Bishop of Meath, Glennon's home diocese, at the time Glennon stopped in Ireland on his way home from Rome, where he had received the "red hat." Soon after he had been greeted by Bishop D'Alton and attended ceremonies in Mullingar (near Hardwood, Glennon's birthplace), the new cardinal died in Dublin on March 9, 1946, of complications from a cold he had caught while in Rome.

April 15, 1956, was a Sunday. In his letter for the commemorative booklet issued for the occasion, Ritter wrote: "More than 20,000 workers without distinction of race or creed conducted a solicitation which resulted in contributions from over 100,000 persons. Unlike many fund-raising efforts, where the bulk of the money comes from large individual contributions, the gifts of the many are responsible for the success of this drive."

At the testimonial dinner after the dedication, Cardinal D'Alton told the more than a thousand guests of all religions and races, "The measure of your devotion to Cardinal Glennon is clearly evident in the sacrifices which you have made to erect such a magnificent hospital in his memory. You could not, indeed, have raised a more fitting memorial to the Cardinal than a children's hospital, nor one dearer to his heart."

When it opened, the hospital was projected to provide direct medical care for thousands of children annually, with outpatient departments alone designed to handle 20,000 or more patient visits a year. Building it required five prime contractors, sixty-four subcontractors, and a daily workforce of 120 men over three years, or a total of nearly 4 million man-hours of straight-time labor.

The day of the dedication, Mother Concordia, SSM, Superior General, wrote to Ritter:

> *Simply to know that our Beloved Archbishop and the Archdiocese of St. Louis have accepted our past and present efforts to assuage the suffering of our City's sick and infirm is cherished assurance. To have been given the privileged task of administering the Cardinal Glennon Memorial Hospital for Children is a token that we almost hesitate to accept, so sacred is its import. That we prove worthy of the confidence with which parents and guardians will place their children in our care is our prayer this evening as it has been our prayer ever since Your Excellency told us that we had been selected to conduct the Hospital.*

A**n aside to the hospital story** involved Bishop John Kyne, D.D., Bishop of Meath, Clonard House, Mullingar, Ireland, who accompanied Cardinal D'Alton on his trip to St. Louis. Archbishop Ritter viewed him as a potential source for priests and sisters on a lend-lease basis from Ireland to St. Louis. In July 1956, Ritter joined some priest friends from Boston on a visit to Ireland and wrote to Kyne beforehand expressing his hope to visit him at Mullingar. Having missed him, the archbishop wrote on August 17 indicating his disappointment, and then added:

> From time to time the thought has come to me that Your Excellency might be able to help us with our shortage of School Sisters. It is becoming more and more of a problem to find Sisters to staff our schools even in part. If I could arrange either for a foundation or for a group of Sisters who would remain attached to their home foundation in Ireland, I think it would be a fine thing not only to supplement our present needs but for the future... [I] would be happy if we could look forward to at least a beginning for the Fall term of 1957, the Sisters coming perhaps several months earlier to get located.

Arrangements were made for both sisters and priests to come, the first contingents arriving in the late fall of 1956. On December 11, 1956, Ritter wrote to Kyne: "The good nuns are doing nicely and we are happy to have them with us. Perhaps they are a little homesick but I don't think too much. The two fine young priests are adjusting themselves and we are all very much impressed by them...My thanks and appreciation to our distinguished benefactor and friend, Your Excellency."

When Kyne recalled one of his priests, Father Andrew Farrell, in the spring of 1962, Cardinal Ritter wrote to thank him. "You may be sure, dear Bishop, that we are deeply grateful both for the services of Father Farrell and your continued interest in our need in St. Louis by sending two priests on a temporary mission for three years."

And so it was that the Diocese of Meath, which had sent John Joseph Glennon to Kansas City, Missouri, in 1883, from whence Pope Leo XIII moved him to St. Louis as coadjutor archbishop in April 1903, more than fifty years later was again supplying personnel to the diocese which that pioneer had served so well.

MEDIA SAVVY

Ritter always had "a nose for the news" and understood the value of media coverage. On October 10, 1954, he gave a talk as part of the inauguration of the first Catholic television program in St. Louis. The program was broadcast on station KWK-TV and sponsored by the Archdiocesan Council of Catholic Men. He thanked the station for affording the Church of St. Louis such an opportunity, and continued, "I want to commend the station for its vision and its interest in the community, for surely a religious program will give much to the moral and spiritual well-being of a community."

That day the *Great Crusade* series began, followed in July 1955 by *Look, Listen and Learn,* itself replaced in September by *We Believe.* In June 1956, *Quiz-A-Catholic* began and ran until October 1966. As television expanded, so did possibilities for its use. The archbishop created the Catholic Radio and Television Apostolate Office to take advantage of this medium of communication; KXOK radio and KMOX-TV were used, as were KTVI-TV, KETC-TV, KXOK-FM, and KMOX radio. The first "live" Mass telecast was on November 1, 1961, with the archbishop as celebrant.

Ritter also paid close attention to the diocesan newspaper. Archbishop Glennon began using the *National Catholic Register* for the diocese in 1940 and it served St. Louis well for sixteen years. On January 1, 1957, the first issue of the *St. Louis Review* was published with Reverend Jasper Chiodini as managing editor. Donald Quinn, a layman and staff reporter, became editor in 1965, taking charge of the paper's editorial pages and covering the Third and Fourth Sessions of the Second Vatican Council. Under Quinn's leadership, the paper twice was judged the best Catholic newspaper in the United States in polls of Catholic journalists.

DESOTO HOTEL

As we have seen, Archbishop Ritter consistently had a heart for those who were disadvantaged and was eager to meet needs as they were identified. Accordingly, in 1956 he purchased the old DeSoto Hotel in downtown St. Louis for use as a home for elderly men and women. It cost $1,500,000, the money coming from the Archdiocesan Expansion Fund. The 300-room building was expected to accommodate 500 guests "without regard to religion or race."

In announcing the acquisition, Ritter said, "The accessibility to all kinds of recreational, social, and kindred facilities will make the residence attractive to a great many people." In June 1956 the Franciscan Sisters of Mary, headquartered in Providence, Rhode Island, arrived to staff the facility, now called the Hotel Alverne. They ran it strictly as a hotel, with maid service, elevator and telephone operators, waitresses, and other personnel. Breakfast and dinner, the two meals served daily, could be had for $2.00 each in 1958. A resident priest offered daily Mass in the chapel, located on the ground floor with its doors opening onto the street. A reading room and convert-instruction program were soon added, making it a center for prayer and conversion in the heart of the downtown district. Both were used extensively by people working in the adjacent offices and other places of business.

**Cardinal Ritter with members of the Hotel Alverne "Kitchen Band,"
June 14, 1965.**

At the same time Ritter bought a modern office building at 4140 Lindell to bring more of the archdiocesan agencies and bureaus under one roof. On arriving in St. Louis, there were nine agencies and bureaus; by 1956 there were eighteen. He also obtained an apartment building at 4396 Lindell and converted it for temporary use for chancery purposes. It was later replaced by a very contemporary chancery office, built on property directly adjacent to the Cathedral rectory. It quickly became known as the "round house."

Ten-Year Mark

At the ten-year mark of his service in St. Louis, Archbishop Ritter was asked to state his goals for the years ahead. He listed three:

- "The...population shift from city to suburban life must be faced and met. It means constant planning and building out from the city.
- More...accommodation for parochial schools, especially high schools. [He built four new ones and thought he had done a good job, but found the need almost unending.]
- The field of planting the Word of God is most fertile in the rural areas. There is a tremendous need for more facilities and for more spiritual work in those areas."

At the beginning of 1956, the Archdiocese of St. Louis had 1,048 diocesan and religious priests, 297 parishes, and 475,000 Catholics. July 1956 would see a decrease to 966 priests, 229 parishes, and 415,000 Catholics, as Missouri Catholics were reorganized into the four dioceses of Jefferson City, Kansas City-St. Joseph, St. Louis, and Springfield-Cape Girardeau. The St. Louis Archdiocese was reduced to the city and county of St. Louis and nine adjoining counties.

March 1958 marked Ritter's twenty-fifth anniversary as a bishop. A group of priests suggested that the occasion be honored with a collection to build a chapel at the new St. Louis Preparatory Seminary South high school. Parishes were asked to give the amount of their annual cathedraticum (chancery tax) from their funds "without any public announcement of the fact." Priests were asked to give the equivalent of one month's salary. The money was collected; in due time the chapel was built and dedicated to St. Joseph.

Public recognition of the anniversary was a Mass of Thanksgiving offered at Kenrick Seminary on Thursday, March 27, followed by a dinner in the refectory. By March 3, $158,518 had been pledged or given by 348 priests and 165 parishes.

CENSUS

The *St. Louis Review* of May 30, 1958, contained a pastoral letter from the four Missouri bishops: Archbishop Ritter, Bishop John Cody, Bishop Charles Helmsing, and Bishop Joseph Marling, C.PP.S., announcing a statewide survey of the Catholic population, "The Missouri Catholic Census Program." Its purpose was to learn "what the needs and resources are" in order to better care for the members of the Church. The census was scheduled for Sunday, September 28. On that day, a force of 30,000 laymen made a door-to-door census of every dwelling in the state. The Metropolitan Federation of Churches, the St. Louis Lutheran Pastoral Conference, and the Rabbinical Association of St. Louis all indicated they would urge their constituents to welcome census takers.

The results showed that, in the archdiocese, the county and outstate Missouri had larger Catholic populations (percentage-wise) than the city, that one of every twelve adult Catholics in the archdiocese was a convert, and that 80 percent of Catholic children attended Catholic grade school or high school. The census set the number of Catholics in the archdiocese at 481,202. A final summary report was given to the archbishop in November 1959. The assistant pastor of Holy Cross Parish in north St. Louis listed several good results of the census in his report:

+ Setting up catechism classes for children in public schools
+ Establishing a Guild of St. Paul for converts
+ Organizing the parish into thirty neighborhoods, each with a patron saint and captain to watch over and respond to needs
+ Making visits to urge parishioners to join the Society for the Propagation of the Faith
+ Forming thirty study groups using the Code for Parents of Teenagers as the basis for discussion

National Shrine of the Immaculate Conception

Archbishop Ritter was invited to give the dedication sermon at the National Shrine of the Immaculate Conception at Catholic University in Washington, D. C., on November 20, 1959. After construction had lagged for many years, Ritter was credited with giving the project the push it needed for completion. He had become a member of the episcopal committee of the shrine in the spring of 1953, at the same time he assumed membership on the Catholic University Executive Board. At the shrine committee meeting it was decided that a national collection should be taken up in all the parishes of the country on December 6 in anticipation of the Marian Year scheduled for 1954.

Building the shrine had begun in 1914 with plans for completion in 1954, the centenary of the proclamation of the Immaculate Conception by Pope Pius IX. Archbishop-Bishop John F. Noll of Fort Wayne had served as chairman of the shrine committee until he suffered a stroke in 1954, when Ritter replaced him. Of the 131 dioceses in the United States in 1958, only six had collected more money for the shrine than St. Louis. The deadline for completion was not met, but the bishops decided to proceed with the dedication in 1959.

In preparation for the November 20 event, Ritter asked the parishes in St. Louis to offer a triduum of prayer with at least the Litany of Mary and a prayer for her help each day, with an act of consecration to Mary Immaculate on the last of the three days. In his sermon he quoted an excerpt from the Pastoral Letter from the twenty-five bishops gathered for the Sixth Council of Baltimore in 1846: "We exhort you, brethren, to continue to cherish a tender devotion to the Mother of our Lord, since the honor given to her is founded on the relation she bears to Him, and is a homage rendered to the mystery of His Incarnation. The more highly you venerate her, as the purest and holiest of creatures, the deeper sense you manifest of His divinity."

Despite obstacles, the shrine was completed, and the main building was the seventh largest Christian church in the world—after St. Peter's in Rome; the cathedrals of Seville, Milan, and Cologne; and the churches of St. John the Divine in New York and Christ Cathedral in Liverpool, England.

EDUCATION ADVOCATE

Archbishop Ritter was totally and fiercely dedicated to Catholic education. On January 10, 1959, he answered Maurice J. Sheehy, C.M., of St. Rose of Lima Parish, Silver Lake, Missouri, who had written seeking permission for students of his parish to attend Sunday morning religious instruction rather than going to the regional Catholic schools. Ritter replied:

wow

> *If transportation is being provided for the children of St. Rose of Lima Parish to attend a Catholic school whether high or grade school, parents are obliged under pain of mortal sin to send their children to the Catholic school. This is a law of the Church and not my law. You must, therefore, as Pastor, refuse the sacraments to these people and bring them to the realization of the seriousness of their responsibilities before God.*

In June 1960 he sent a directive ordering that Catholics in the St. Louis Archdiocese could not attend secular colleges without written permission. In his directive he noted that permission would be granted only when parents and students promised that the latter would participate in Newman Club programs at the school. Part of his confidence in taking this position arose from the ready access for young men and women to Catholic colleges in the St. Louis area: Saint Louis University, run by the Jesuits; Fontbonne College, conducted by the Sisters of St. Joseph of Carondelet; Maryville College, under the direction of the Madames of the Sacred Heart; and Webster College, staffed by the Sisters of Loretto of Nerinx, Kentucky.

As the college ranks began to swell with children of war veterans, St. Louis was in an advantageous position to offer a full Catholic education at every level from grade school through the university, and the archbishop believed that young people should make full use of the opportunities available to them.

Accolades

In honor of his leadership and great influence in the cause of education, on March 23, 1961, Saint Louis University bestowed on the archbishop the honor of "Founder of St. Louis University." It was the first time this honor had been conferred since the very early days of the institution. Very Reverend Joseph Fisher, S.J., the Jesuit provincial, and Very Reverend Paul Reinert, S.J., the school president, made the presentation to Ritter both for his work in Catholic education and his support for the university in pursuing its mission as an academic institution dedicated to handing on and promoting the Catholic faith.

Joseph Cardinal Ritter (left) receiving a citation declaring him a founder
of Saint Louis University in March 1961. Presenting the award are the
Very Reverend Joseph P. Fisher, S.J., provincial of the Missouri Province
of the Society of Jesus, and the Very Reverend Paul C. Reinert, S.J.,
president of the university.

Meeting the Needs of Older Priests

As large classes of priests were ordained for St. Louis from the 1940s through the 1960s, conditions of priestly life and service changed. Rectories became crowded and the average life expectancy of their occupants grew. Formerly, elderly priests retired and continued to live in their last place of assignment, but as their numbers increased, it was necessary to seek alternate solutions to a developing dilemma: how to provide appropriate retirement facilities for priests seventy-five years of age and older, as well as those retired because of illness or other reasons. The solution must provide for their material needs while at the same time offering their usual sacerdotal companionship.

Archbishop Ritter took a bold step in addressing this challenge. On April 29, 1958, he authorized the Congregation of the Sacerdotal Fraternity, in Ottawa, Canada, to establish an institution in St. Louis. They came to manage Regina Cleri, an apartment building that the archdiocese had purchased at 4540 Lindell, a block west of the New Cathedral, to respond to this need.

The Congregation and its counterpart, the Sisters of the Congregation of the Oblates of Bethany, were founded in France for the express purpose of caring for retired and infirm priests. Members of both Congregations arrived in June 1958, and during the next year several priests had entered Regina Cleri, affectionately called "Ritter's Hilton." On March 24, 1960, the diocese gave the property to the Congregation of the Sacerdotal Fraternity with the stipulation that if they should ever leave, it would remit to the diocese.

All went well until 1966, when a split within the sisters' community and unwise financial management threatened to divide the members of the Congregations: sixty-five priests, fourteen seminarians, seventy-five brothers, and 207 religious sisters serving in St. Louis and in Europe and South America. The communities weathered the storm and continued their work in St. Louis with notable success for another twelve years, when they had to leave because of a decrease in their own numbers. The management of the home then fell to the Catholic Charities Office of the archdiocese.

A Second St. Louis Synod

Archbishop Ritter called for another synod, this in November 1960, the second under his jurisdiction and the ninth in the archdiocese. As in 1950, the

Synod IX

preliminaries of a notice to all the priests, an invitation to choose a deanery representative for the synod committee, plus an invitation to offer recommendations, were again followed.

The synod was held at Kenrick Seminary and began with a procession into the chapel followed by a Pontifical Low Mass.

The clergy section of the synod statutes began, "Your bishop wants a renewal of vigor and of spiritual beauty in his Diocese. At the center of this renewal is the person and the life of the priest. His person is sacred and his life must be holy," a quote from Pope John XXIII on the occasion of the Roman Synod held earlier in 1960.

Among the statutes was one that said: "Religious brothers and sisters are not allowed to attend secular schools within the archdiocese without our permission." Another noted, "The subject matter of the Sunday sermons will follow the systematic program of instructions distributed by the Chancery," a clear recognition that the Sunday readings, which the Church had been using each year basically unaltered since 1570, had by overuse been drained of their power to inspire. A related statute read: "Sermons and public addresses given by the clergy or visiting priests in the diocese or elsewhere are subject to our examination upon request."

Salaries were set at $1,800 per year for pastors; $1,200 for assistants with ten or more years in service; $1,080 for assistants with less than ten years of service; and for religious teachers: $1,200 for an M.A., $1,000 for a B.A., and $800 for those with no degree. Male teachers were paid $1,500.

Among the 264 statutes was also this: "Permission to perform a mixed marriage in church, under the usual conditions, is automatically given with the granting of the required dispensations, except during the seasons of Lent and Advent." This removed the cumbersome process of having to apply in each case for permission to celebrate such marriages in church rather than in a parlor of the rectory.

One on Sunday Mass began: "The Church today urges a fuller participation of the faithful in the liturgy of the Mass." Together with an adequate instruction for the people, it called for a longer time for Masses, so that a ninety-minute separation was decreed for the last three Masses on Sunday at each parish, with none to begin after noon. If necessary, parishes could celebrate an evening Mass on Sunday after 4:00 PM. In a bow to the growing awareness of Catholic Action in the Church of the twentieth century, the final statute called for priests "to channel capable men and women imbued with the social principles of the Church into the vital fields of communications, management and labor, social work, teaching and government."

Disconcerting Times

The early 1960s were a time of explosive growth in the American Catholic Church. Parishes expanded, school systems were enlarged, seminaries for priests and novitiates for religious sisters and brothers were built in record numbers. But the Vietnam War and the assassination of President Kennedy raised a dark cloud on the horizon that even the Second Vatican Council could not totally dissipate. Religious vocation numbers began to decline, and some of the facilities built to foster them had to be used for other purposes. Even with its wealth of religious communities with headquarters in St. Louis, the archdiocese suffered from this reduction, especially as the expansion of high schools continued at a rapid pace.

The Question of Married Priests

In the years after World War II, Pope Pius XII, who had been the papal nuncio to Germany in the 1930s, permitted a number of married German Lutheran and Evangelical pastors who had joined the Catholic Church to be ordained priests. In St. Louis on Easter Sunday of 1953, Monsignor Martin B. Hellriegel, pastor of Holy Cross Parish in north St. Louis, received into the Church two Lutheran pastors, Irvin Arkin and Ernest Beck, together with their families.

Dr. Arkin opted for a career as a university professor at Saint Louis University, but Ernest Beck wanted to be ordained a priest. In 1961 Monsignor Hellriegel wrote on Beck's behalf to the Sacred Congregation for the Discipline of the Sacraments seeking his ordination. The Most Reverend Zerba Cesare, Secretary of the Congregation, contacted Ritter about this request and Ritter answered expressing his admiration for Beck and his family for the sacrifices they made in becoming Catholics. However, since Beck was married and had children, the archbishop believed that his wish to be ordained should be subordinated to the good of the Church of America. Ritter wrote that the clergy and faithful and even non-Catholics had a high regard for celibacy of the clergy, and any exceptions would diminish their regard. Ritter acknowledged the precedent that had been set for Germany regarding such ordinations but felt it would not lead to many conversions in the United States.

Beck then applied to Bishop Mark Carroll of Wichita, Kansas, and later to Richard Cardinal Cushing of Boston, both of whom explored the matter without success, although Beck insisted that he had been given a verbal permission for ordination by Pope Pius XII in a private audience. Finally, Archbishop Jaeger of Paderborn, Germany, did ordain him. He served as pastor to American Catholic military personnel at Wiesbaden Air Base for several years, until he and his family moved to the Diocese of Raleigh, North Carolina, to take up pastoral duties there.

Archbishop Ritter handled the matter well. He could have expressed chagrin that one of his priests would write about such an issue to Rome without consulting him first, but he chose instead to deal with the question directly. Perhaps his respect for Monsignor Hellriegel, who had studied at St. Meinrad Seminary during several of the years Ritter was there and had become one of the leading proponents of liturgical renewal in the Church, overrode any feelings of annoyance he might have experienced.

5

Mission
Focus

One of the glories of the Archdiocese of St. Louis was its historical role in sending missionaries to the American West. Father
Pierre-Jean De Smet, S.J., was the most renowned, but a host of other
priests and religious, including Saint Rose Philippine Duchesne, were
sent from "the Rome of the West" to evangelize Indian tribes and offer
spiritual support to Catholics seeking their fortunes in newly opened
territories beyond the Mississippi River. St. Louis had a strong tradition
of supporting missionary ventures.

Archbishop Ritter was no less dedicated to the missions. His first letter
to the priests of St. Louis, dated September 13, 1946, was in fact issued from
Indianapolis. It concerned the annual collection for the missions on Sunday,
October 20. In it Ritter said:

> On Mission Sunday itself, we direct that a special mission sermon be
> preached in all the Masses throughout the Archdiocese. An outline will
> be furnished by the Propagation of the Faith Office to provide sugges-
> tions for the sermon, but you yourself must breathe into the sermon the
> life of your priestly zeal and love for souls. The people should be asked
> to receive Holy Communion on this Sunday. No one can inspire them
> to generosity and love better than our Blessed Lord Himself.

Ritter encouraged missionary promotion in the archdiocese. In 1951 on the Feast of All Saints he visited the seminarians at Maryknoll House and told the students:

> *It is necessary for us to be saints and the first step is to desire holiness. We must ask our Lord through his Blessed Mother to give us the gift of sanctity. We must be holy and live as a holy man would. Holiness is based upon obedience. This desire and cooperation with grace through obedience become the foundation of the sanctity which is so necessary for any priest at home or in the mission field.*

Archbishop Ritter hosted a World Mission Exhibition in St. Louis from Sunday through Thursday (May 17–21, 1953), sponsored by the Society for the Propagation of the Faith and the Association of the Holy Childhood. More than 250,000 attended. The event began with a Marian procession through the streets of downtown to the Soldiers' Memorial, but hail and a rainstorm broke up the march. Nevertheless, an estimated crowd of 60,000 people assembled in the four-block square for the Pontifical Mass celebrated at 3:00 PM. Police estimated that it was the largest religious gathering in the history of St. Louis.

Archbishop Ritter blesses the crowd during a procession before the Mass for world peace in downtown St. Louis. The procession and Mass were two of the ceremonies marking the opening of the Archbishop Ritter World Mission Exhibition, sponsored by the Society for the Propagation of the Faith and the Association of the Holy Childhood. (RELIGIOUS NEWS PHOTO SERVICE)

Bishop Fulton J. Sheen, national director of the Society for the Propagation of the Faith, delivered the closing talk in the Kiel Auditorium. On February 23, 1954, he sent a letter to Auxiliary Bishop Charles H. Helmsing, the local director of the Propagation Office, congratulating him on "the most successful of all Missionary Exhibits" and on the creation of the "Daily World Missionaries" (DWM), one of the outcomes of the Exhibition. The DWM was simple in the extreme: members put aside a quarter a day and sent the money once a month to the mission office. The few meetings for members were motivational in character. Over the years the program generated enough money to make St. Louis the highest-contributing diocese, per capita, in the entire country. Sheen called the DWM "the most modern, most complete and up-to-date approach to mission aid that has ever been developed."

Bolivia Mission

Thomas J. Danehy, M.M., Vicar Apostolic of Bolivia, had just been consecrated a bishop on April 22, 1953, at Manitowoc, Wisconsin. He attended the Exhibition and visited with Ritter, discussing with him the possibility of sending priests to Bolivia on a missionary basis. The next year this request was followed by a formal invitation from the Apostolic Nuncio, Archbishop Umberto Mozzoni, to send priests to serve in an area of the capital city of La Paz, which at that time was part of the San Pedro Parish. The Nuncio laid down a number of conditions:

+ The St. Louis diocesan priests would establish a new parish in the area mentioned. San Pedro counted more than 80,000 people in its boundaries.
+ The St. Louis priests would have the support of the Maryknoll Fathers who had arrived in Bolivia in 1942. They had a center at Cochabamba, which served as a language school for their missionaries newly assigned to Bolivia. The St. Louis priests were welcome to avail themselves of Maryknoll's facilities.
+ Since the Maryknoll Fathers had accumulated several years of experience in Bolivia, their advice could be helpful. They also spoke English, were from the United States, and culturally closer to the U.S. diocesan priests.

Some time later, at the request of Archbishop Abel Antezana of La Paz, Pope Pius XII issued a general appeal for help in reducing the numeric gap between the priests and the people of the Bolivian capital. Ritter responded by sending a letter to sixty St. Louis priests who had been ordained five to ten years, inviting them to consider serving in South America; forty responded. To further explore the implications of this undertaking, he wrote to Padre Juan Kostik, C.PP.S., pastor of a parish in Chile:

> *You will be surprised to learn that the Archdiocese of St. Louis is plan-*
> *ning to send Diocesan priests as missionaries to Bolivia, the request*
> *having been made by the Nuncio. The Maryknoll Fathers, too, have*
> *a vicariate there and they have encouraged us in the undertaking.*
>
> *Accordingly, I plan to send two or three priests during the month*
> *of May and for a year or two they will take up residence in parishes*
> *in [the] charge of American missionaries such as yours no doubt. This*
> *will enable them to learn the customs of the people and to obtain a*
> *better knowledge of the use of the language. I would like for you to tell*
> *me what type of priests I should send. There are quite a number who*
> *have volunteered—to my great surprise—and of course from them I*
> *will choose the first three to go.*
>
> *I am sure this will be a great surprise to you and I know give you*
> *great happiness too because you are aware of the need for priests in*
> *South America, and if the dioceses of the United States will open up*
> *and take part I think we can make a wonderful contribution. It seems*
> *the Nuncio in Bolivia is especially anxious that parishes along the lines*
> *of those here in the United States should be set up as the people have*
> *no idea of parish life nor the priests for that matter.*
>
> *I suppose the men will be assigned by the Archbishop to parishes*
> *in La Paz or some of the larger places.*

After consulting with others, Padre Postik wrote on March 2, 1956:

> *The answer is always the same. "He better come prepared to like the*
> *South Americans or at least not to despise them." Unless he can swal-*
> *low his dislikes he might as well stay home. The Bolivian or Chilean is*

different from the American only in accidentals, and in some people's minds the accidentals are everything. A Latin is proud, subtle, and always ready to take advantage of you. But the Latin may be very humble, too, and very simple, and will give of himself without stint... The second qualification a missioner should have is patience. He should not expect a blossoming American style parish within 50 or a 100 years...In South America one has the few rich, the multitude of poor, a fair sprinkling of the middle class which breaks its own neck by trying to keep up with the rich...In Chile a parish U.S. style is quite an impossibility. We have to work to get the people to church, to think "Catholic" and not "class," and then we will have the parishes. Of course, a missioner must be a man of God, and as such—provided he has the qualifications of "all things to all men" and "patience," he need not be a linguist (my neighbor a Maryknoller was here 20 years and speaks a horrible Spanish, but he is one of the best to be had, his people love him), need not be a luminary, need not be a hustler, just a common sense priest.

With solid advice from those in the mission field and a large list of St. Louis priests who had volunteered, Archbishop Ritter resolved to send men to Bolivia in what he later described as "the most important decision of my life." The three chosen were Fathers Andrew Kennedy, David Ratermann, and Andrew Schierhoff.

Father Kennedy traveled to La Paz with Bishop Charles Helmsing, director of the Propagation of the Faith Office in St. Louis, to work out the contractual details with Archbishop Antezana, while Fathers Ratermann and Schierhoff gathered items they would need for their work. The departure ceremony was held at the St. Louis Cathedral on Pentecost Sunday, May 20, 1956. In his comments Archbishop Ritter said: "Today the Church in the United States has come of age."

U.S. Diocesan Priests as Missionaries

Sending archdiocesan priests from St. Louis to Bolivia was not the first time American diocesan priests were sent to a foreign mission. In 1841, in response to a plea from the Second Council of Baltimore (1833), the Vicar General of Philadelphia, a New York priest, and a Baltimore layman left for missionary work in Liberia. They were Monsignor Edward Barron, Reverend John Kelly, and Denis Pindar. Liberia had been established on the West African coast in 1821 by the American Colonization Society as a settlement for freed U.S. slaves and it became an independent republic in 1847. The Society transported 6,000 slaves between 1821 and 1867. The American bishops felt some responsibility for those who had received Catholic baptism and sent the three to minister to them in their new country.

On May 23, 1956, the three new missionaries were on their way. They traveled by ship to Arica, Chile, and from there by train to La Paz. After studying Spanish with the Maryknollers at Cochabamba for two months, they took up residence in a rented house near the center of what would become the parish of Christ the King. The first public Mass was celebrated in the open air on August 30, in those days the feast of St. Rose of Lima.

In December 1956, Archbishop Ritter visited the mission to see firsthand the living conditions of the people his priests were serving. He flew to La Paz, the first ordinary of a diocese in the United States ever to visit Bolivia. The mission itself was the first ever directly established and supported in a foreign country by a single American diocese. Ritter also visited a group of Brothers of Mary from St. Louis who were then stationed in Lima, Peru.

In this effort, Ritter was ahead of his time. The Second Vatican Council in 1964 in its Dogmatic Constitution on the Church would call on the world's bishops to "come to the aid of the missions by every means in their power, supplying both harvest workers and also spiritual and material assistance." The archbishop of St. Louis anticipated this by almost twenty years. Other bishops imitated his example. In 1962, after he had become the bishop of Kansas City-St. Joseph, Missouri, Bishop Charles Helmsing, a former auxiliary bishop of Ritter in St. Louis, opened a parish in Bolivia.

He also recruited and sent numerous lay papal volunteers to Latin America, and at one point his diocese had the highest percentage of papal volunteers of any diocese in the United States.

On May 17, 1962, Ritter wrote to Albert Cardinal Meyer of Chicago in support of an appeal from Bishop Prata, auxiliary of La Paz, for funds for priests there:

> *He is not asking for priests but he wants to raise the economic conditions of the native Bolivian priests. They seldom have rectories to live in and their income is almost nil. They see the discrepancy now between their condition and ours since our American priests, supported by their home dioceses, are in their midst and it is creating a bad situation. In raising the economic standard of living among the clergy it is the Bishop's conviction he will raise their standard of pastoral work and also effect an increase in vocations to the priesthood.*
>
> *It seems to me that this is a very sensible and practical approach and helping him is even better than sending your priests. I know Chicago has done much already for Bolivia as we have done but I hope you will find your way to encourage the Bishop in his difficult work. The old Archbishop has assigned Bishop Prata as his special work the parishes of the Archdiocese. Already the native clergy are reacting favorably since at last someone is becoming interested in them.*

A year later Ritter received a communique from Archbishop Romolo Carboni, Apostolic Nuncio in Peru, dated April 30, 1963. He wrote:

> *My private opinion is that the Church in Latin America is beginning to gain momentum in Her struggle to pull herself together and move ahead against their enemies. But the fight has just begun, the advances costly and slow, and the road a long one. However, I believe that we are proceeding in the right direction. While the church here is optimistic, it is realistic to know that it needs help and lots of it.*

In September 1963, Ritter once more visited Bolivia, this time as a cardinal of the Church. He was officially received at the La Paz airport by Church leaders, including nine St. Louis priests, and was publicly welcomed by President Victor Paz Estenssoro, representatives of the Bolivian army, and state department heads. When he visited Viacha, "Thousands lined the streets: brass bands played, women wept, children threw flowers. Veteran political observers, accustomed to seeing mixed reactions to United States statesmen on their trips to South America, said they had seen nothing like it in their whole experience."

In Viacha, where three priests had opened and reconditioned a four-hundred-year-old church, the cardinal was met on the outskirts of the town by a jeep bearing an episcopal throne draped with Indian blankets that had been woven especially for the occasion. Three bands—one of townspeople, two from military units stationed nearby—accompanied the procession with Ritter atop the swaying jeep throne as it went through the crowded streets amid a shower of confetti to St. Augustine Church. The next day the cardinal celebrated Mass for the whole town. Returning to La Paz, he received from Estenssoro the Bolivian "Grand Cross of the Condor of the Andes," the nation's highest decoration.

Joseph Cardinal Ritter acknowledging the greetings of Aymara Indians during a 1963 visit to Viacha, Bolivia, to missions supported by the St. Louis Archdiocese. (AP NEWSFEATURES PHOTO)

Back in St. Louis after the five-day trip, Ritter's first comment was, "I think people are getting so tired of me coming back, they wish I'd stay home." In a twenty-minute interview at the airport he said:

> *St. Louisans, even non-Catholics, should be highly gratified over the wonderful contribution the missions are making to the social as well as religious health of Bolivia, because it reflects credit on our city as a whole. The work of the St. Louisans who staff our missions—nine priests, some dozen Sisters, and five lay volunteers—is received with great admiration by the Bolivian people and government alike.*

He noted that Bolivia was having its own civil rights problem, but the situation was the reverse of our nation because the underprivileged Indians constituted the majority of the population, not the minority. He also observed:

> *They want to raise themselves to make Catholicism the official state religion in Bolivia, and that necessarily involved me in a great many activities in connection with the respect due to my position as a Cardinal and a representative of the Holy Father. We don't have that sort of thing (state religion) here, and I'm just as happy about it that we don't have it. Observance of the protocol requires a great deal of effort and time.*

MISSION EXPANSION IN SOUTH AMERICA

By the spring of 1964 there were ten St. Louis diocesan priests serving parishes in La Paz and nearby Viacha. Twenty papal volunteers were working in a number of South American countries under the sponsorship of St. Louis. In April plans were announced for staffing a third South American parish, this time in Arica, Chile. Bolivia continued to request help. On May 3, 1965, Archbishop Carmine Rocco, Apostolic Nuncio to Bolivia, wrote to Ritter from La Paz asking help for a new facility "to house the blind, deaf and other mental cases." Monsignor Drumm, the chancellor, answered in the cardinal's absence and declined: "The Archdiocese has received more appeals from the whole world than we can take care of at the present time."

In April 1967, Cardinal Ritter summed up his views on missionary work south of the border in these words: "If a priest going to South America wants to introduce American ideas, American customs or institutions in South America, he is going to waste his time and somebody's money that's given to him."

6

Promoter of
Ecumenism

St. Louis was singularly blessed with strong religious leaders in the
first half of the twentieth century. Cardinals John Glennon and
Joseph Ritter, Episcopal Bishops William Scarlett and George Cadigan,
African Methodist Episcopal leaders Vinton Anderson and George
Stevens, Presbyterians Sherman Skinner and James Clark, and Rabbis
Julius Gordon and Ferdinand Isserman all played significant roles in the
city and the larger community beyond it.

In the mid-1950s, Congregation Temple Israel decided to move from
Washington and Union Avenues in the west end of St. Louis out to a new
location on Ladue Road in Creve Coeur. Its board applied for authoriza-
tion to build a new temple there, but the request was denied by the city. The
congregation took the issue to court and, after a long battle, won its case.
Archbishop Ritter instructed the archdiocesan lawyers to enter a friend-of-
the-court brief on behalf of the congregation. When the new building was
dedicated in 1959, the congregation presented a scroll to Ritter in appreciation of his support of their efforts.

When ecumenism came up for debate at the First Session of Vatican
Council II, Cardinal Ritter supported the movement on the floor of the Council. The day he returned to St. Louis he attended an ecumenical meeting at

Kenrick Seminary. The *National Catholic Reporter* asked him to describe the background of that meeting. He responded, "First, small groups held regular meetings. Then there were larger meetings—the first was at Eden Seminary with the Protestants as hosts, and then we Catholics were hosts at our Kenrick Seminary…These meetings have been enjoyed…and both priests and ministers seem to get a lot out of them."

In February 1963 he addressed religious leaders of area churches and synagogues when he spoke at the St. Louis Advertising Club. In his remarks he proposed a new definition of "church":

> "Certainly there is only one Church, and that is the Church of Christ. Certainly it can take on a spirit of reunion and this is what we hope for. Certainly all of us can review our position, and I think this is a healthy sign. Religion is not a static thing; it varies. Of course, the doctrine doesn't vary, but the teachings must be constantly updated to our times. Christ not only spoke to the Church 2,000 years ago. He is speaking to it today. And, therefore, a definition of the Church is needed."

> He referred to Pope Pius XII and his encyclical letter Mystici Corporis Christi of 1943, where he used Pauline concepts to describe the Church as the Body of Christ. "There are all kinds of members in the human body and all are essential. So also with the Body of Christ. All Christians throughout the world…are essential to bring out the teachings of the Church. Christ is the Head and we are the members. We all constitute the Church. We are all necessary to constitute the Church," he concluded as he gestured to include the 575 persons in attendance.

On another occasion he said:

> No one can foresee when unity will be brought about. It is pretty much in the hands of God. I believe that the Council and the more ecumenical spirit on the part of non-Catholics is creating a climate which will enable the Holy Spirit to do his work. Almost everyone is now aware of the need for union. Different groups have different ideas of how this

should be done. But with prayer and desire, no one can say that unity will not be accomplished in the near future. Surely the world situation religiously will hasten unity.

As an Episcopalian clergyman from Washington said recently, it is possible that the Council will force the Protestants to face this challenge...It is not intended to be a challenge, of course, but is so developing that we can no longer hide behind our prejudices. We have...to face each other and discuss our differences—this is so essential to the peace of the world. A united Christendom is so vitally needed. The fact that Christendom has been divided may account for its weaknesses and for the world situation...But Christianity is growing stronger.

In June, three leaders of the Episcopal Church—Bishop George Cadigan; Dr. Clifford Morehouse of New York, President of the Episcopal House of Deputies; and Reverend W. Murray Kennedy of St. Mark's Church in St. Louis Hills—visited Ritter. They invited him to address a major session of the convention of the Episcopal Church in the United States in St. Louis in October 1964. Bishop Cadigan later wrote, "We were saying our good-byes to the Cardinal and it seemed right to suggest that he give us his blessing. When we rose, he very quietly said that he would be honored if we gave him our blessing. This humility brought tears to my eyes."

Cardinal Ritter's practical experience in ecumenism and his recognition of its importance prompted him to take a strong stand in supporting the schema on ecumenism at the Vatican Council II, according to a communiqué issued by the Vatican Press Office on November 8, 1963. He told the Council Fathers:

> *The present schema is an answer to the need for explaining the practical consequences of the AGGIORNAMENTO, which is the aim of the Council. The presentation of this text marks the end of the Counter Reformation and obliges us to make a thorough examination of conscience. Likewise it puts us under obligation to hasten the desirable day of unity by fervent prayer, example and study. Without a declaration of this kind by the Council, there can be no mutual discussion and the door will be closed to any real dialogue with those outside the Church.*

Such a declaration should not be based upon motives of expediency. It should proceed from solid theological principles, namely, (1) the absolute freedom of the act of faith, (2) the inviolability of the human conscience, and (3) the incompetence of any civil government to interpret the Gospel of Christ, with consequent independence of the Church from civil authority in the accomplishment of its mission. In the text, greater attention should be paid to the celebration of the Eucharist as a symbol of unity, and the importance of the liturgy. There should be also a clear affirmation of the validity of the sacraments and the orders of the Oriental Church. The text should be cleared of expressions offensive to Protestants. There is no valid reason for denying the use of the term "church" to the religious groups which originated in the sixteenth century.

Like any other living movement, ecumenism is subject to dangers. Excessive intellectualism can make it sterile and it can easily likewise degenerate into indifferentism. This is why we need a VADEMECUM, or practical directives, which will provide safe guidance.

VATICAN II TERMINOLOGY

aggiornamento

Aggiornamento, which means "bringing up to date," was one of the key terms during the Second Vatican Council and was used by bishops, clergy, and media attending the sessions. The word was used to mean a spirit of change, openness, open-mindedness, and modernity.

Pope John XXIII used the word to describe the Church's need to renew and update itself through the Second Vatican Council.

aula

Aula is Latin for "hall"; during Vatican II the nave of St. Peter's Basilica was known as the *aula*, the place where the council deliberations were held.

vademecum

A *vademecum* is an authoritative handbook or reference standard by which Catholics may know the truths of the faith.

St. Louis clergy depart for the Second Session of Vatican II in September 1963. From left, Reverend Nicholas Persich, C.M.; Bishop George Gottwald; Joseph Cardinal Ritter; Monsignor George Lodes; and Monsignor Joseph Baker.

Because the point was not expressed in the official communiqués as clearly as he wished, Ritter released a text of his intervention in the Council's *aula* to the Divine Word news service, operated by Father Wittgen, who, in turn, issued a press release on November 21, 1963. The release emphasized that the cardinal considered "religious liberty as the basis and prerequisite for ecumenical contacts with other Christian bodies," and urged the inclusion of an unequivocal declaration on religious liberty in the schema on ecumenism. He further asserted that "whether or not the Fourth Chapter on the Jews strictly pertained to the schema on ecumenism," he was nevertheless highly pleased with the decree itself, "which clearly pertains to the goals proposed by this Council."

As the debate became more heated, Ritter made his second intervention on the subject, his sixth of the Second Session according to the official communiqué issued on November 25. In it he said:

> It should be pointed out [in the schema] how the unity which is the goal of ecumenism is a fundamental principle of the ecumenical movement. For this reason the schema should work out a real concept of unity. Our basic inspiration should be pastoral. We are not only issuing a decree, but are also expected to provide with it effective stimulus to action...We have with our separated brethren common desires and common activities. We should present unity not merely as a goal of inestimable value, but in such a way as to show disunion as an evil of equal magnitude. Chapter One presents a concept of unity which only Catholics can recognize. In her present state, the Church is far from the realization of the full perfection which belongs to her by nature. Separation and division in the ranks of Christians are a scandal to the world. The text tells us that such divisions retard the coming Kingdom of God. We shall, of course, be united in perfect unity only when we are together at the Lord's table. We should pray for unity in the recognition of [the] one same truth.

In an earlier talk in 1963 to the Conference of Christians and Jews, he said about the Council:

The invitations sent to our Protestant and Orthodox brethren, their gracious acceptances and their kind words about the Council, show clearly that a new day has already dawned...There will be much dialogue, perhaps even a diatribe here and there, but I am convinced that responsible men on both sides know what to do with dialogue... "Though many, we are one." There are many kinds of unity, some more easily attainable than others. Some forms will have to wait upon the discussions and consultations of experts. But there isn't a person in this room—or in the world, for that matter—who is not qualified to be an expert in matters of mutual respect, trust and understanding. This is the oneness that the Conference of Christians and Jews is striving so heroically to achieve—and may it meet with every success.

Dr. Joseph Lichten, of the Anti-Defamation League of B'nai B'rith, read Ritter's words in the newspaper and approved of them in an interview on November 20, 1963. He observed that Ritter was one of only nine speakers at the Council who spoke on November 18 and strongly praised the need for a declaration against anti-Semitism. Lichten said he was happy to be in the city of "one of the world's greatest friends of Catholic-Jewish cooperation."

In an interview in Rome halfway through the Second Session, Cardinal Ritter remarked: "You can get the statement [against anti-Semitism] perhaps, but it isn't going to change the thinking of the Catholic people—that's what we've got to change. That's not going to be easy. It requires real work on the part of all. The Pope could make a statement and the bishops could issue pastoral letters, but these don't solve the problem: Reform has to take place at all levels, local, diocesan and national."

Shortly after returning to St. Louis, Cardinal Ritter spoke of the Muslim nations' dissatisfaction regarding the chapter in the schema that dealt with the Church's relationship with Judaism. He told a reporter he hoped Pope Paul VI's visit to the Holy Land would "generate discussion" of proposed policy changes concerning Jews and "allay some fears that the Church is endorsing Israel." He said that the Pope's itinerary "will show that he is above all this by including visits to many regions of the Near East. God works with Jews, too. Their hope for salvation is as valid as ours if they are sincere in their beliefs and follow the dictates of their conscience."

Not all Protestant Council observers were positive. Bishop Marling of Jefferson City wrote to Cardinal Ritter on August 13, 1963, asking that Dr. Stanley I. Stuber's invitation to attend be withdrawn. Ritter then wrote to Amleto Cardinal Cicognani at the Vatican requesting that this be done, "if it can be done prudently. The gentleman has used the privilege he had in attending the Council to cover his own bigotry and…aggrandizement. I do not know who recommended him to…Rome."

Local Ecumenical Activity

Ecumenical activities had become part of the St. Louis scene in the 1960s. Between 1961 and 1966 there were six Protestant-Catholic dialogues in the city. The locations included Kenrick and Eden Seminaries and First Congregational Church of Webster Groves. Topics likewise varied from year to year. The final gathering, in 1966, was at Kenrick Seminary and the speaker was His Lordship Dr. John Moorman, Bishop of Ripon, England, an Anglican observer at Vatican II.

On March 19, 1964, Cardinal Ritter formed the Archdiocesan Commission on Ecumenism, which he said "takes note of intense local interest in the movement and of local pioneering ecumenical activity over the past several years." Six days later, Anglican Bishop George Cadigan invited the cardinal to attend the Evening Prayer of the Annual Convention of the Anglican Diocese of Missouri, at Christ Church Cathedral, in April. Ritter responded through his chancellor, Monsignor William Drumm, because he was attending meetings in Washington. Drumm wrote in part: "The Cardinal was honored to be invited and if it were up to him personally, he would readily accept. However, he does not think at this time our people would understand. On the other hand he has greater confidence in your own goodness to appreciate the position in which he finds himself." Obviously Ritter was aware that not everyone was pleased with the advances he was making in ecumenical affairs, some believing he was going too far too fast, others judging his activities as imprudent at best, and threatening to the integrity of the faith at worst.

Nor were the other American bishops always cooperative. In early April of 1964, Ritter sent a telegram to Bishop Jerome D. Hannan of the Diocese of Scranton, Pennsylvania, suggesting that Father John Sheerin might be permitted to attend as an observer, along with a second observer, a conference of the World Council of Churches to be held in Pennsylvania later that month, and that Father Joseph Gremillion be permitted to address the conference.

Hannan replied by quoting a paragraph he sent to Cardinal Bea, head of the Secretariat for Promoting Christian Unity, after receiving the same request:

> *Buck Hill Falls [the location of the conference] has been a source of constant irritation to the faithful of this area. They have regarded the frequent meetings there of influential Protestants somewhat as Protestants view a Eucharistic Congress, as a means of advertising the prestige enjoyed by Protestantism. The resentment with which the faithful have for many years viewed the visits of Protestants to this mountain would assuredly be expanded to include me if I countenanced any degree of participation in a Protestant Conference there.*

Ritter sent a brief telegram in reply: "Your letter received. Am disappointed and regret that it was not more favorable."

GONE BUT NOT FORGOTTEN

As prominent churchmen left the scene, even Protestant ones, they were not forgotten. On May 12, 1964, Cardinal Ritter sent this letter to Right Reverend Arthur Lichtenberger, Episcopal Church Center, New York:

> *Dear Bishop Lichtenberger, I learned from the press that you are retiring as Presiding Bishop of the Church of America because of illness. I want to assure you of my concern and constant remembrance in my prayers. May the good Lord strengthen you and your family in this time of trial and may you receive every spiritual consolation. In union of prayer and with personal regard, I am, sincerely yours in Christ...*

A Mixed Marriage

On June 13, 1964, a wedding occurred in a Catholic church in a St. Louis suburb in which a Catholic priest and an Episcopalian priest officiated together. Susan Ekberg, an Episcopalian, married Patrick Baker, a Catholic. The priests read from the Episcopal *Book of Common Prayer.* The exhortation and final blessing came from the Catholic Ritual. The event gained a great deal of notoriety. On July 27, Cardinal Ritter wrote to Bishop Cadigan regarding the wedding, for which the cardinal had given his permission. "While it was a bit disconcerting to have the wedding given so much publicity, I soon adjusted myself to it and I am sure our good people also have. It is remarkable that the affair should have created such interest. In the long run I hope good will comes from the publicity. In the meantime be assured that I continue as always."

The repercussions of the marriage continued to plague Ritter as the year moved on, as is evident in a letter he sent to a number of bishops on December 29. It read, in part:

> *Also, because I have been urged to do so, I would suggest extreme caution in the matter of adopting rules with respect to new dispositions in the field of interconfessional marriages, and marriages in general, as this could prove highly embarrassing at a later date. I am convinced that the sanctity of the married vocation will be safeguarded more effectively by placing greater responsibility on the contracting parties and placing less trust in signed agreements. At the same time, I feel we must begin to work towards a correction of the grave scandal caused by the frequency of our declarations of nullity for lack of canonical form. These are widely cited as affording a Catholic version of trial marriage.*

He was acknowledging that he might have gone too far in granting permission for the June wedding, but that restrictions concerning marriages of mixed faiths were still causing too many couples to seek civil unions for which a decree of nullity could be easily obtained at a future date.

ADDITIONAL ECUMENICAL EFFORTS

Late in 1964, the cardinal received two invitations. On December 12, Dr. Reuben A. Holden of Yale University wrote to Ritter informing him that the "President and Fellows of Yale University voted to confer on you the honorary degree of Doctor of Divinity." Four days later he replied, thanking him but declining the honor, as was his normal policy. The same day he answered an invitation from Dr. Robert Fauth, President of Eden Seminary, thanking him for his

> …*kind letter of December 16th inviting me to give the Commencement address on June 4, 1965…It is indeed a source of great satisfaction to know that the invitation comes at the unanimous request of the entire Eden faculty. In view of this and also because I have at least the reputation for promoting the ecumenical spirit I can hardly refuse. Accordingly, I am marking my calendar for June 4, 1965, at 8:00 PM, and assure you it will be a pleasure for me to be with you.*

At the request of the World Council of Churches, Cardinal Ritter wrote a short article for use in connection with the Week of Prayer for Christian Unity of January 18–25, 1965. In it he noted:

> *When he receives distinguished visitors, it is the Pope's custom to give a small memento of the visit…At the Third Session, Pope Paul personally chose to give a remembrance better calculated to symbolize our strivings toward Christian unity. The gift he selected was a critical edition of the New Testament printed in Greek and Latin and bound in red leather. As he presented the book to each observer, he told each one of his conviction that it is here in the words of Scripture that the basis for our dialogue is to be found…I share the same persuasion.*

In early January the cardinal sent out three sermons on ecumenism to be preached in each parish on the second through fourth Sundays after Epiphany. The last sermon contained this conclusion:

> *One of the most profoundly moving events of the Second Vatican Council took place at the opening of its Second Session on September 29, 1963, when Pope Paul, in the midst of his opening address, turned to the observers from other Christian communions and declared "Our voice trembles and our heart beats faster both because of the inexpress-*

ible consolation and reasonable hope that their presence stirs up within us as well as because of the deep sadness we feel at their prolonged separation, if we are in any way to blame for that separation."

Cardinal Ritter gave the promised address at Eden Seminary on June 4, 1965, and chose as his subject "The Seminary in an Ecumenical Age." He concluded with these words:

Finally, in the irenic spirit of this occasion, I should like to address a few words to the members of the graduating class. It is my belief that here at Eden you have been exposed to a vital and challenging Christianity. I congratulate you upon the completion of your course and I don't think it will compromise my position to add that I pray for you. I pray that you will carry to your ministry the ecumenical spirit of this institution. I pray that you will be truly bearers of God's Word to the people you serve, which is a way of saying the same thing; and where you find Christians asleep to the challenges of our time, I pray that you will be disturbers of the peace. God bless you.

This was an extraordinary moment in the history of denominational relations in St. Louis. To have the leader of the Catholic community address the students of a Protestant seminary in a nonpolemical way, and even with strong words of encouragement for those poised to begin their service in God's vineyard beyond the confines of Catholicism, was a giant step forward in interdenominational affairs.

The address was a major success and received wide coverage. On June 17, 1965, Ritter responded to a letter from his former auxiliary, Bishop Charles H. Helmsing of Kansas City-St. Joseph, who was also the episcopal chairman of the Ecumenical Commission and office of the National Conference of Catholic Bishops.

I have just received your letter and thank you for your kind observations regarding my talk at Eden Seminary. It is, as you no doubt can surmise, mostly Monsignor Baker's work. Monsignor is aware of the fact that it would be well to send a copy of the talk to the Secretariat and if he has not already done so I will send it as you suggest. You are absolutely right in expressing the fear that we may lose by hesitant and timorous disciplinary action what the Council has freely given. You can speak from personal experience.

Earlier in the month he had sent Helmsing a word of encouragement after the latter had apparently received a note advising caution from the Secretariat in Rome:

Really the Secretariat needs the example of initiative, such as yours, to build up its positive action. There are so many who are so terribly fearful of all such encounters, that in spite of the beautiful decree on ecumenism, there is the danger that disciplinary action take back what the Fathers of the Council have so generously given us. I can tell you that in our latest meeting in Rome your guidelines for ecumenism were given very serious and heartfelt approval. Since we are all so new in the ecumenical movement, it is important that we have practical demonstrations of what can be done and what is being done with full faith and perfect charity within the framework of what the Council has decreed.

On August 4, Bishop Loras T. Lane of Rockford, Illinois, sent a letter congratulating the cardinal "on the address Your Eminence gave on 'The Seminary in an Ecumenical Age' at the Eden Theological Seminary. Your remarks made a timely contribution in putting the ecumenical movement in proper focus. I particularly enjoyed your excellent treatment of that which lies at the very heart of the ecumenical movement, the Eucharist. May the address of Your Eminence help to hasten the day when we can all unite in one common faith around the table of the Lord."

Ritter replied on August 9: "I appreciate your kind letter of August 4th more than I can express in this letter. With so many brickbats coming my way an occasional pat on the back from a highly regarded friend is more than comforting." Clearly there was not universal approval among the hierarchy either of what he had said or that he had given the talk at a Protestant institution.

After he returned from the last session of the Second Vatican Council in December 1965, he received a letter from Walter F. Wolbrecht, Executive Director of the Lutheran Church-Missouri Synod:

> *I am particularly grateful for the many kindnesses shown me and my colleagues, Doctor O. C. J. Hoffman and Doctor Carl S. Meyer, by you and the members of your staff during the…Session of the Vatican Council. We are grateful to the Blessed and Holy Trinity for having brought you safely back after the rigors of the Council and its special demands for leadership made to you and met by you. As you said to me in our delightful luncheon shortly before I left Rome: "The proof of the Council will be in the coming months and years to come."*

The cardinal replied: "Be assured that your presence and that of your colleagues coming from St. Louis to the Council pleased me very much and it was very easy to place myself and my associates, Monsignor Baker and Father Persich, at your disposition. It was a wonderful event if for no other reason than bringing us closer to each other."

More Praise for Ecumenical Spirit

Other persons prominent in the ecumenical movement joined the chorus of praise for Cardinal Ritter's efforts on ecumenism at Vatican II. On December 6, Walter B. Price, Executive Director, Missouri Council of Churches, wrote: "Dear Cardinal Ritter, We greet you in the name of Jesus Christ, our one Lord and Savior. We welcome you home to our state of Missouri and to our common task of service for God, our heavenly Father. We congratulate you for the tremendous ecumenical achievement which has been accomplished in Rome for the total Church of Jesus Christ. May the blessing of God the Father, His Son, our Lord and Savior, bring you peace and joy during this holiday season and throughout the coming year."

A telegram dated December 23 read: "Welcome home. Thank you for many things, but particularly for what you are. Christmas greetings and God keep you." George L. Cadigan (Bishop of the Anglican Diocese of Missouri).

And another read: "Welcome home. Congratulations on having given great leadership to enlightened causes. Seasons' greetings." Rabbi F. M. Isserman, December 24, 1965.

Ecumenical promotion was one of Cardinal Ritter's highest achievements. His success was due to his profound conviction that Christian unity was at the center of God's will for the world, and to his willingness to take a lead in reaching out to fellow Christians on an equal basis. In his mind and actions he evidenced the belief that efforts expended in the cause of unity, founded on prayer and mutual respect between partners pursuing the goal together, would lead to its ultimate achievement. As he said in his last public interview: "The ecumenical spirit is growing. I don't think anything can stop it. Now, how long it will take to bring about a real union, that is in God's hands, but it may come more quickly than we realize."

7

Installation as Cardinal

On December 14, 1960, Archbishop Ritter received a personal letter from Pope John XXIII notifying him that he been nominated to be a cardinal. Two days later Ritter spoke to the press about the nomination:

> *While it is indeed a great personal honor, it is also an honor to St. Louis to which I am glad to belong. I have been exceedingly happy in St. Louis during the past fourteen years since my coming and I rejoice in being able to add ecclesiastically to the luster of its name. It is also an honor for the Church of St. Louis, its people, religious and devoted clergy. They, with me...are thinking of Cardinal Glennon who, through his long tenure of pastoral work and leadership here, first brought this distinction to St. Louis. My receiving the honor now gives me a sense of satisfaction in that I am walking in his traditions and share in the same dignity.*

Ritter was indeed continuing Glennon's work: he had raised more than $125,000,000 during those fourteen years to build forty-one new parishes, sixteen high schools, and Cardinal Glennon Memorial Hospital for Children.

Many had speculated that he would receive the red hat earlier than he did. Glennon's tragic death on his way home from Rome in 1946 and the burial of his body in the Cathedral crypt on March 16 left the people of the archdiocese with fond memories but no leadership. Many thought that once Rome filled the see with a new archbishop, he would quickly be elevated to the rank of cardinal to compensate for the loss. However, this was not to be. Pope Pius XII made no move in that direction, and Pope John XXIII did so only in the fourth consistory of his reign. Others felt that, although there had been cardinals for 1,500 years, only sixteen Americans had received that honor before Ritter, and St. Louis did not deserve the same consideration as New York, Boston, Los Angeles, and Chicago.

However, as James Johnson, author of *Men Who Made the Council*, later wrote:

> *Overshadowed in the eyes of the public by the Cardinals of the East—the powerful Spellman in New York and the colorful Cushing in Boston—Cardinal Ritter is nevertheless the most consistent, systematic, reflective leader of the modern renewal in the American Church. Honest, open, devoted to the Gospels, Cardinal Ritter has become in the eyes of bishops of the world the most respected of the American prelates of his generation, and in the eyes of his people in St. Louis a pastor in the spirit of Pope John.*

Asked to describe the cardinal-elect's personality, one aide replied: "He has a warm, wonderful sense of humor. He's an affable man, one who asks for no special consideration. He eats what we eat. If it's hamburger, he eats hamburger." A slight man of 150 pounds, he was at his best in small groups. His soft-spoken humor was reserved for the privacy of the luncheon table at the archiepiscopal residence at 4510 Lindell, a half block from the chancery office, where he dined daily with colleagues and poked fun at them and himself.

A writer for the *St. Louis Globe-Democrat* noted about Ritter:

> *Not an outstanding orator in the pulpit, he is regarded as most effective when he is conferring with small groups. A personal warmth which seeps through to those he seeks to influence adds to his effectiveness. He possesses the human touch in large measure. He maintains personal contact with hundreds. In patient longhand, he writes numerous letters of condolence or congratulations.*

When his brother, Dr. Harry Ritter, received the news of Ritter's elevation to cardinal, he commented: "This would have been a grand thing for [our]
parents. Mom would have been overwhelmed. She cried when he became a
bishop. Dad would have taken it coolly." The "baker's boy" had made good.

TERMINOLOGY

consistory

A *consistory* is a formal meeting of the Sacred College of Cardinals of the
Catholic Church, except when the cardinals are convened to elect a new pope
(then the name is a *conclave*). Consistories are held in Vatican City to take care of
the business of the college, which usually involves advising the pope on important
matters concerning the Church.

Family members joined the planeload of bishops, priests, and laypeople
who flew with Ritter to Rome. His sister Catherine, a Sister of Charity of
Nazareth, Kentucky, and his niece Mary Martha, a Sister of Loretto of Nerinx,
Kentucky, went as his personal guests. A sister-in-law, Helen Ritter, and her
daughter, also named Helen; his brother Carl's widow, her son and daughter
and son-in-law; a first cousin and her husband, two daughters, and a son-in-
law were all part of the entourage traveling to the Eternal City.

In a press notice issued from the chancery office before he left the city,
the cardinal-elect said: "We all realize that honor brings responsibility, and
therefore, while rejoicing with the good people of St. Louis, I must look to
them, the wonderful Catholic people, to the devoted clergy and religious of
the Archdiocese, as well as to all St. Louisans, to help me by their prayers and
cooperation in meeting the challenges which lie ahead."

The party departed St. Louis on Tuesday, January 10, 1961, and arrived in
Rome the next day. On Thursday they attended Mass at St. Peter's, followed
by sightseeing. On Friday they went to St. John Lateran and on Saturday to
St. Mary Major, with more sightseeing each day. Sunday was a free day. On
Monday the "Biglietto" ceremony took place at the North American College

with the presentation of the formal decree (the *biglietti* are the formal written notices of elevation to the rank of cardinal) from the Sacred Consistorial Congregation. It was followed by personal visits from cardinals stationed in Rome or who had traveled there for the consistory. Tuesday was again a free day. The ceremonies in Rome were arranged to the smallest detail, and booklets outlining them and giving the necessary directions were provided for each new cardinal and his group.

Joseph Elmer Ritter receives the red hat from Pope John XXIII.

who?
4

On Wednesday, January 18, the red hats were bestowed on the four new cardinals. Ritter, as senior of the four, thanked the Pope for the honor given to them.

> *Your great goodness and condescension which constantly extends to all parts of the world seems at this moment to be addressed in particular to the two Americas. Two of us, in fact, are from South America (Jose Cardinal Quintero, Archbishop of Caracas, Venezuela; and Luis Cardinal Concha Córdoba, Archbishop of Bogota, Colombia). I am from North America, and His Eminence Giuseppe Cardinal Ferfetto, although of Italian nationality, is closely bound to our religious life in as much as he has worked diligently and fruitfully on the Commission for Latin America of which he is the Secretary… In certain areas of our continent religious needs require help from every side, so that they may be met quickly and efficiently. Above all, it is more than essential that one America extend a helping hand to the other America, its sister through the nobility of a common name, so that both together can push away the common threat and dangers with even greater strength in the observance of the Catholic Faith and law.*

Cardinal Ritter was the first American to act as speaker on the occasion of the bestowing of the red hat. The pope thanked the cardinal "for the noble and considered words which you have expressed to us in the language of Rome" [Latin]. He went on to note that the four cardinals he created brought to his mind the four faces on the wheels of Ezekiel's chariot. They are wheels, he said, "which go forward, which move around the throne of the Almighty, directed only toward His glory, toward carrying forward the fiery chariot which in contact with the earth is transformed into a flame of charity."

Official portrait of Joseph Elmer Cardinal Ritter. (CHASE LTD., PHOTO. WASHINGTON, DC.)

Cardinal Ritter was appointed a member of the Sacred Consistorial Congregation, the Sacred Congregation for the Propagation of the Faith, and the Sacred Congregation for the Basilica of St. Peter. He was proclaimed a Cardinal Priest of the Holy Roman Church under the title of Most Holy Redeemer and St. Alphonsus on the Esquiline Hill. His titular church was officially "Church of the Most Holy Redeemer and St. Alphonsus Liguori," commonly called "Sant' Alfonso." It is located on a busy shopping street called Via Merulana, just a block south of St. Mary Major. Above its main altar stands the original portrait of Our Lady of Perpetual Help. Daubed (not painted with brush strokes) in a tempera process on hard wood, the painting is only sixteen by twenty inches in size, and is thought to date to the twelfth century.

The new Cardinal Ritter takes possession of his titular church of Sant' Alfonso in Rome.

On Thursday, January 19, the St. Louis contingent enjoyed an audience with the pope, who told them, "Love this man. Love him and follow him." Three days later Cardinal Ritter took possession of his titular church and celebrated the Eucharist there for the first time. The travelers left for home on Tuesday, January 24. After returning to St. Louis, Ritter sent money to repair and redecorate Sant' Alfonso.

Cardinal Ritter was officially welcomed back to St. Louis at a noon Mass at the Cathedral on Sunday, January 29. On February 7 the cardinal celebrated Mass at Kenrick Seminary for the priests of the diocese. At the dinner that followed, the clergy presented him with funds they had collected to be used for the education of priests.

The civic community honored him with a dinner on February 10. When President John F. Kennedy was informed of the honor Ritter had received, he was reminded that in 1950 they had together received honorary Doctor of Law degrees from the University of Notre Dame. He sent a telegram to be read at the gathering: "I am delighted to add a message to the testimonial for Cardinal Ritter. This occasion recognizes his outstanding community leadership and personal influence. Cardinal Ritter's life and work stand out as one of the finest achievements in guiding a whole community to new standards of excellence and human concern."

Governor John Dalton of Missouri gave a speech at the dinner in which he said: "Cardinal Ritter, by his daily life and his participation in the affairs of the community, is putting into actual practice the teaching of the Old and New Testaments. I believe this is the basic reason why persons representing so many different groups and religions in this community can unite as they have in paying their respects to [him]."

Fourteen hundred guests attended, including members of Protestant and Jewish congregations who joined with others from municipal, county, and state agencies.

On April 30 the cardinal visited his hometown, New Albany, Indiana, to preside at a Eucharist at Saint Mary's church. The solemn High Mass was celebrated with an overflow crowd, and 2,000—including old classmates—attended the afternoon reception held at the parish school. In his remarks that day he said, "I'm a born Hoosier and I'm proud of it." When he was named a cardinal he sent a message to the people of Indianapolis: "I could not forget you. When word came of this great honor, I thought of you who helped me to merit it. Surely you are my joy and crown."

Among the episcopal greetings Cardinal Ritter received were the following:

- "I wish to express my appreciation to you for the cordial kindness of yourself in so many ways to me personally and to the various problems in which I have involved you through the years" (Thomas Gorman of Dallas-Fort Worth).

- "It is a valid and fitting recognition of all your accomplishments for God and Country during the many years of your illustrious service to the Church" (Thomas Connolly of Seattle).

- "I have been greatly edified by Your Eminence's perfect record of attendance at the meetings of the Executive Committee of The Catholic University no less than by the practical way you always took of matters presented to it" (Jerome Hannan of Scranton).

- "The thought keeps popping back into my mind over and over again that you must have been one of those appointed in petto a year or more ago. I am inclined to think that you were aware of this appointment at the recent Bishops' Meeting in Washington" (George Rehring of Toledo).

- "It was a tremendous source of joy to hear yesterday afternoon that Our Most Holy Father had conferred upon you the great honor of being a Cardinal of Holy Mother Church. My heartfelt congratulations and prayerful good wishes that God's choicest blessings will be yours. Buon natale and kindest remembrances with deep appreciation for your goodness to me" (John J. Carberry of Lafayette in Indiana, who would succeed Ritter in St. Louis).

- "We in Bolivia owe a great deal to Your Eminence's pioneering interest in the problems of the Church in Latin America. The news of your elevation was something we have looked forward to for some time" (Charles A. Brown, auxiliary bishop of Santa Cruz de la Sierra, Bolivia).

*   Perhaps the most touching came from Richard Cardinal Cushing of Boston: "My Dear Archbishop: Congratulations. I thank God I have lived to see this honor of a Prince of the Church conferred on you! *Nunc dimittis servum tuum, Domine* [Now dismiss your servant, O Lord!]"

The cardinal's coat of arms had two mottos: one above the shield reading "Ipsa Duce Non Fatigaris" (Guided by Her You Will Walk Without Weariness), taken from the second nocturne of the feast of Holy Name of Mary, found in the Roman Missal in English, and the motto used by Bishop Chartrand, who ordained the cardinal in 1917 for the Diocese of Indianapolis; the other was "Miles Christi Sum" (I Am a Soldier of Christ) from Saint Paul's Second Letter to Timothy (2:3).

The cost of his cardinal robes was $3,403.60 and included forty-four separate items ranging from $2.80 to $825.00. As he donned his robes for a picture for the *St. Louis Globe-Democrat,* he quipped: "I mustn't pretend I know how all this goes on. People will say, 'See, that fellow has been practicing a long time.'"

8

The Second Vatican Council Years

Part One (1962 and 1963)

On January 25, 1959, Pope John XXIII announced his intention of convening a general council. At first there was widespread surprise and, for some, even consternation, but further thought led many to conclude it was gravely needed. Communism, Nazism, and Fascism were all twentieth-century movements that began in supposedly Christian nations. Two terrible world wars were waged in a period of thirty years, the second spilling out from Europe to engulf much of the Northern Hemisphere. The horrific trench warfare from 1914 to 1918, the Holocaust, the wanton bombing of cities, and the unthinkable destruction wrought by atomic bombs dropped on Hiroshima and Nagasaki in 1945 were all clear manifestations that Christianity had lost its capacity to influence world events. A "renewal of the face of the earth" was decidedly needed. The pope courageously challenged the Church to face the world squarely and energize it with a fresh spiritual vision.

**Cardinals McIntyre, Cushing, Spellman, Ritter, and Meyer
at the North American College in Rome.**

He convoked the Council on December 25, 1961. The following spring, he appointed Cardinal Ritter a member of the Pontifical Preparatory Commission, which was to meet in Rome on June 12. The cardinal arrived there the day before, accompanied by Father Nicholas Persich, C.M., a dogma professor at Kenrick Seminary. Before leaving, Ritter on May 23 wrote to Cardinal Meyer of Chicago, urging him to attend the June meeting of the Pontifical Commission because of his background in Roman affairs and his theological qualifications, noting that "the Bishops of the country are expecting us to be there representing them." He was determined to enter the uncharted waters of this enterprise with commitment and dedication and was hoping that others would do so with equal enthusiasm.

His experience at the June Commission meeting impressed upon him the seriousness of what would occur when the 2,600 bishops of the world gathered in the Eternal City, and of the need for prayer to the Holy Spirit for guidance if the Council was to have any success. So in preparation for the Council, he directed that a novena to the Holy Spirit be conducted in every parish of the archdiocese in September of 1962. Priests were assigned on a pulpit-exchange basis to preach a set of sermons issued by the chancery office, the talks to be given in the context of prayer and Benediction of the Blessed Sacrament.

Pope John XXIII instructed that the "Constitution on the Sacred Liturgy" be the first document discussed. It had turned out to be the best of the original seventy-three documents prepared and the subsequent seventeen presented for discussion. The debate on the liturgy schema lasted for fifteen sessions, from October 22 until November 13. Cardinal Spellman, the first American to speak, took a conservative line, arguing for the preservation of Latin as the language of worship.

Cardinal Ritter spoke the next day and his comments reflected the liturgical movement that had been developing in Midwest America for two decades. After quoting the Council of Trent on the Church's responsibility to institute rites and ceremonies and to change them as it judged expedient, he urged acceptance:

> *Venerable brothers, it seems to me that the schema…is admirable for*
> *its aptitude, rectitude and prudence…To reject this schema is to reject*
> *an accommodation so great that it would, in fact, negate the very great*

changes which, through all the ages, obtain a place in the life both of the world and the Church...In this century we have come a long way toward recognizing the practice of the rights and offices of Christ's faithful as members of the Mystical Body of Christ...We must render possible this fuller participation which is the right and office of the laity and accommodate the liturgical decrees to actual conditions...

When the debate began regarding the Dogmatic Constitution on the Church, Ritter was the first American to speak. He claimed that the schema was "entirely inadequate." He criticized its containing nothing about the sanctity of the Church; its neglecting to stress the duty of all members, including the laity, to preserve the deposit of faith; and its statement of principles about Church-state relations that no longer had any value. He then offered his own conception of the Church:

The Church is Christ Himself mystically living and working in all the members, in whom the Holy Spirit—the Spirit of Christ—dwells and operates...In Christ, through Christ and with Christ the Church teaches, offers worship, sanctifies and is sanctified and in some way rules and reigns. Every member has a part in activities of this sort and in the life of the Church—each according to his own talents.

Ritter's intervention, together with those of Cardinals Liénart, Frings, Léger, Koenig, Suenens, and Bea, doomed the work the Theological Commission had done in preparing the schema. Cardinal Ottaviani of the Holy Office and his supporters defended the schema as presented, but it became clear that a large majority of the Council Fathers were dissatisfied with it. Pope John XXIII directed that the schema be given for consideration to a Mixed Commission of members from the Theological Commission and Secretariat for Christian Unity so that it might reflect the emerging twentieth-century understanding of the Church that began with Pope Pius XII's groundbreaking encyclical letter of 1943 on the Mystical Body of Christ (*Mystici Corporis Christi*).

On his return to St. Louis, Ritter was complimented for his willingness to offer interventions on the Council floor, resisting the steamroller tactics of some of the conservative Council Fathers. He replied, "Our own fellows were not talking about what we believe here in the States. I guess it got my Dutch up. I got up and I talked."

In subsequent sessions, the American bishops moved from a basically conservative stance to one which was more open as bishops from other continents and cultures made known the needs of the Church in their countries and dioceses.

In the first days of 1963, Ritter learned that Cardinal Bea had been invited by Cardinal Cushing to give a series of lectures in the United States. It alarmed him because Bea had some health problems and he considered him a key person in the life and deliberations of the Council. He wrote to Bea on January 3 and—while apologizing for his boldness—asked him to decline the invitation because it "would be a tremendous strain…an ordeal that might possibly, at your age, have serious consequences." He thought Bea would better serve the Church if he stayed in Rome to maintain his health and work toward the next Council Session.

Contrary to Ritter's recommendation, Bea did give the series of lectures without any injury to his health. Ritter tried to regain some lost ground with the cardinal by sending him a short note expressing his disappointment at his not being able to visit St. Louis, since plans called for him to speak only in Boston and New York.

Cardinal Ritter acted in good faith; it would have been a catastrophe if Bea had suffered a setback to his health. The more liberal forces of Vatican II would have lost one of their chief leaders, and several documents of the Council might have been significantly different without Bea's influence and guidance. The fact that Ritter felt free to write to Bea in the manner he did suggests that he had become very much at home in the inner circles of the Council and thought he could express his views with confidence that they would be considered in a serious way without being offensive. His subsequent relations with Bea indicated that such was the case.

Ritter gave a report on the First Session to a gathering of priests and Protestant ministers at Kenrick Seminary in which he said:

I am not a relative of Father Martin Luther, or of King Henry the Eighth, but after listening to John XXIII in Rome, I returned home

*an enthusiast for the reunion of Christendom…My hope now is that
the Curia in Rome will be confined to executive work while the Holy
Father and Bishops frame the administration of the Church…In my
judgment, the National Catholic Welfare Conference with American freedom has built the most successful and powerful branch of the
Catholic Church in the world.*

In January, Bishop James V. Casey of Lincoln, Nebraska, invited Ritter
to dedicate at a later date a religious institution then under construction. In
doing so he also included a word of thanks: "Several of us, sitting back on
the 'five-yard line' [at the Council] had reason to be most grateful to you for
the leadership you gave in several critical matters. [I hope] it will continue
during the next session."

Ritter replied on February 4: "I never dreamed I would do any talking
in the Council when I went over. I must say, however, I was challenged by
being reminded of my predecessor in the First Vatican." He was alluding
to Archbishop Peter Richard Kenrick of St. Louis, who staunchly and
persistently opposed the doctrine of papal infallibility supported by the great
majority of bishops gathered for Vatican Council I and promulgated by Pope
Pius IX just prior to the suspension of that Council due to the outbreak of
the Franco-Prussian War in 1870. To avoid going on record as voting against
the doctrine Kenrick left Rome on the day the vote on it was taken.

On February 12, the cardinal addressed the Advertising Club of
St. Louis, and he began by noting that in Rome the speeches were limited to
ten minutes and delivered in Latin, but here, he presumed, "I'm to be permitted to address you in English." He told the group that during the First Session
there were thirty-six general or business sessions, 630 addresses, and 685 additional interventions turned in to the office of the Secretary. Some Fathers
were "strict" and others "permissive" in their approach, but both attitudes
sprang from "the deepest love" for their people. "I look back on the days of
the Council with a special fondness when I recall that seated directly across
from me—in an honored place—were the observers from other Christian
denominations. Savoring such a moment I give thanks for the understanding,
Christ-like heart of Pope John and Cardinal Bea whose labors did so much
to make this possible."

On February 16 one of his Council aides, Father Nicholas Persich, C.M., wrote him a strongly worded letter to protest actions taken at Catholic University in Washington. Father Godfrey Diekmann, O.S.B., was a patristics scholar of St. John's Abbey in Collegeville, Minnesota. Persich had gotten to know him in Rome where Diekmann was serving as an advisor to the group working on the Council document on liturgy. Diekmann had been on a rotation for teaching at the university every third summer and was a popular lecturer there. In the fall of 1962 Father Gerard Sloyan, head of the Department of Religious Education, wrote to Abbot Baldwin of St. John's to confirm Diekmann's appointment for the summer of 1963 and all was arranged.

But in February 1963, Sloyan had to retract the invitation. Monsignor William J. McDonald, rector of the university, notified Sloyan through a third party that Diekmann "should be good enough not to join us this summer." Apparently Diekmann had spoken publicly in favor of using some vernacular in the liturgy. That was presumed to be in conflict with the Apostolic Constitution On the Promotion of the Study of Latin (*Veterum Sapientiae*) of Pope John XXIII encouraging a greater use of Latin in the study of theology in seminaries. The issue was further aggravated when Monsignor Joseph McAllister, vice rector of the university, announced that Diekmann, Hans Kung, John Courtney Murray, S.J., and Gustave Weigel, S.J., all of them renowned theologians, were being removed from the list of potential speakers for a Lenten lecture series to be sponsored by the university's graduate-student council.

In his letter Father Persich, considered at Kenrick a mild-mannered Thomistic professor and dean of men, wrote these fiery words:

> *For Catholic scholars in general, for the ordinary Catholic, and in particular for the Protestant observer, the recent ban imposed upon four respected scholars by the Rector of the Catholic University and what will follow will speak much more forcefully about the Church than will all the glowing accounts of what the Second Vatican Council has achieved and what it will accomplish. To my mind, Your Eminence, if the American Bishops permit the present situation in Washington to continue and develop, they will be betraying the very spirit of the Council.*

TERMINOLOGY

peritus

Peritus is Latin for "expert" and is the title given to theologians who give advice at an ecumenical council. At Vatican II, some *periti* (the plural form) accompanied individual bishops or groups of bishops from various countries. Others were formally appointed as advisors to the whole Council.

Ritter had relied heavily on Persich's advice at the Council; now he read with alarm his observations on this matter and decided to address it himself. On February 19, as a member of the University Board of Trustees, he wrote to the rector:

> *I am profoundly dismayed that the officials of a citadel of learning could fail to realize the slur to the reputation of these four eminent and orthodox priests by ruling them unacceptable "at this time."…I believe that the Spirit of the Second Vatican Council has been compromised by this decision. It is tragic that, at the very time Pope John has led the Church into an ecumenical dialogue, the Catholic University has shown unmistakable signs of fear over an exchange of views among Catholics….A great institution must uphold its tradition. (The Monk's Tale, p. 200.)*

Part of the fallout of this episode was that Diekmann was not invited to the Council as a *peritus* until May 1963, when Archbishop Paul J. Hallinan of Atlanta notified him that he had been named a *peritus* to the Commission of the Sacred Liturgy.

In addition to Ritter, others recognized that this was an issue of importance, and comments from across the country voiced support of Ritter's action:

- Reverend J. A. O'Brien of the Bureau of Convert Research at the University of Notre Dame sent a note to Cardinal Ritter dated March 29: "Just a line to say how indebted we all are to you for raising your voice in protest against the ban at the C.U." The dispute received national attention.

• Bishop William Connare of Greensburg, Pennsylvania, wrote on April 5: "I read with keen interest the Time article a week ago, airing the Catholic University controversy. I was delighted to see your part in the unfortunate affair...You have helped to set the record straight for the good of the Church, which stands to suffer as much as the University from such short-sighted policy...It might seem presumptuous of me to add that we who are a little younger, look to you for guidance and direction in these critical days for the Church...We like your approach and feel it will best advance the best interests of our people, who, when all is said and done, are the Church."

• Two days later Monsignor John Tracy Ellis wrote: "Last Monday evening I took dinner with the president of a Catholic college in the Middle West and he remarked that a bishop had recently told him that during the first session of the Vatican Council the leadership of the American hierarchy that emerged was clearly lodged in the hands of Your Eminence and Archbishop Hallinan. This was the third time I had heard this statement. I thank Your Eminence for the enlightened interest which you showed in recent events here (at Catholic U.), and in saying this I am voicing, I know, the sentiments of almost the entire teaching body of the University. So frequently we have felt the need of understanding and support from those highly placed in the Church and so frequently, to be very frank, we have been disappointed."

Cardinal Ritter's protest was motivated in part by the fact that he had invited Dr. Kung to St. Louis to give a Clergy Conference entitled "The Church and Freedom." The intended audience was a joint gathering of priests, seminarians, and Protestant and Orthodox clergy at the St. Louis Preparatory Seminary on April 20. The plan included another presentation, a week later, to 8,500 attendees of the annual convention of the National Catholic Education Association at Kiel Auditorium. Following the talk to the administrators, principals, and teachers, Father Paul Reinert, S.J., President of Saint Louis

University, bestowed on Kung his first honorary degree of Doctor of Laws (LLD), declaring him to be a "man of vision."

At the clergy meeting Kung was impressed that "the kind, highly-educated cardinal sits in the midst of all these Catholic and Protestant clergy in simple priest's clothing." Father Kung had gained a measure of renown through his book, *The Council, Reform and Reunion*, which had proven extraordinarily prescient in its vision of what the Council agenda would be. He was also serving as a *peritus* to Bishop Leiprecht of Rottenburg when the Council was in session.

Pope John XXIII, who had been suffering from stomach cancer, died on June 3, 1963. His death was a terrible loss both for Catholics and people of all faiths. Cardinal Ritter received numerous expressions of sympathy from religious leaders in the St. Louis area:

+ Bishop Cadigan sent a telegram: "The Episcopal Diocese of Missouri shares with our Sister Communion your loss of a great and holy man."

+ Father Constantine J. Andrews sent a letter: "The Church Board of St. Nicholas Greek Orthodox Church and the Greek Orthodox people of St. Louis join me in expressing deep sadness on the passing away of the Holy Father Pope John XXIII. We join our Roman Catholic brethren in their hour of mourning for their spiritual leader, who in the short span of almost five years did so much for the world at large, as well as his own Church."

+ Dr. W. Sherman Skinner sent a telegram: "The hearts of Christians and all men of good will are saddened at the passing of his holiness, Pope John 23rd. On behalf of the Metropolitan Church Federation of Greater St. Louis and a host of individual Protestants permit me to express to you and the people of the Archdiocese our genuine sympathy and profound sorrow at the loss of a great spiritual leader."

+ Rabbi Magence sent this telegram: "Together with all people around the globe we the officers and members of Beth Tephilah Congregation [in St. Louis] moan the great loss of a great spiritual leader, humanitarian and man lover. In his short reign as Pope he wrote many great pages of history. Men and mankind will never forget this devoted man to all."

Cardinal Ritter went to Rome for the burial and remained with the other eighty-one cardinals who met in conclave to elect the next pope. He was the first St. Louis prelate to participate in such an event. The cardinals gathered on June 19 with the first ballot the following day. On the fifth ballot they elected Giovanni Cardinal Montini of Milan, who took the name Paul VI. There had been fear that the cardinals would not choose a progressive pope, but Vatican II had already moved them to a more open view of church affairs. An article in the *St. Louis Post-Dispatch* of June 5 had noted, "Cardinals Cushing and Ritter became the darlings of the American press here at the Council last fall. Cardinal Cushing for his willingness to meet and speak with reporters, and Cardinal Ritter for his efforts to open up sources of information for them. Archbishop Hallinan opened a crack in the line and Cardinal Ritter carried the ball through for us."

Second Council Session

The Second Session of the Council opened on September 29, 1963. The first debate centered on the Dogmatic Constitution on the Church. Cardinal Ritter spoke on October 3 and recommended that the document include a strong statement on "a theology of the Word of God, living and efficaciously working in the Church of Christ. Word and sacrament, with ruling power, comprise the salvific and sanctifying ministry of the Church. 'To preach' and 'to teach'—conceptually these activities are almost synonymous with the Church."

Eleven days later he spoke again on the same document, focusing this time on episcopal collegiality and pointing out that Scripture and tradition needed to be included to present a full treatment of the subject. On November 5 the amended schema on bishops reached the Council floor after having been drawn up primarily by members of the Roman Curia. The Council Fathers were not happy with the results. That afternoon at their regular meeting, the American bishops had a lively discussion concerning episcopal conferences, with the general feeling being that they should vote favorably for the schema as a basis for discussion so that the matter could move forward. Two days later

Ritter addressed the Council in the name of many other American bishops and stated that the actual necessities of the Church "demand that the powers of resident bishops in many matters be amplified," acknowledging that doing so would be difficult and could only be fully achieved through the revision of the Code of Canon Law. Then, speaking in his own name, he said: "The Roman Curia exists only because it is delegated by the Roman Pontiff," and that the document should indicate that even in the titles of its chapters.

A rumor circulated in Rome that Ritter was also going to speak in the name of the American bishops, who were generally in favor of the restoration of the diaconate as a permanent stable rank. A Council *peritus* (Father Nicholas Persich) narrated that Cardinals Cushing and McIntyre "got together" and discouraged him from doing so. "It was a case of two Irishmen against a German." But in an interview, the cardinal said he saw no reason why older men, particularly retired persons, and even younger men and papal volunteers should not be ordained. "In mission countries younger married deacons might be needed, although some have argued that it would cost too much to support them and their families. But there are catechists there and their families have to be supported. I don't see what difference this argument makes."

On November 14, Cardinal Ottaviani presented on the Council floor the schema on the sources of revelation, and the debate caused much dissension, as 105 Council Fathers spoke. Ritter said the schema must be rejected; Cardinals Léger, Koenig, Alfrink, Suenens, and others agreed. Ritter cited as reasons for his position that, first, the schema contained nothing new from earlier debate; second, there was no accommodation to making either Christian doctrine or Christian life of greater significance for modern man; and, finally, "nothing is said that is clear and determined," the whole schema being clouded with pessimism and a negative spirit. He concluded, "Let the Council abstain from statements that lack any use, imperil unity and engender suspicions."

On Monday, November 18, during the sixty-ninth congregation of the Second Session, Amleto Cardinal Cicognani introduced the schema on ecumenism. Cardinal Ritter was the first American to speak, and did so not only for himself but for many of his American confreres. He was pleased with the schema, "because it responded well to the necessity of expressing the practical consequences of the *aggiornamento* of the Church." He called it "the final end of the counter-reformation with its unfortunate polemics," and welcomed it because "it urges us to hasten that day in which all will be one in Christ through prayer, study, dialogue and action."

Of the five distinct observations he made, the most pertinent was on religious liberty:

> *Since we consider religious liberty to be the foundation and prerequisite for ecumenical relations with other Christians, we strongly urge that the tract on this subject be incorporated into the schema before a consideration of the practices of ecumenism....We must incorporate considerations on the freedom of the act of faith, on the dignity of the human person and his inviolable conscience, on the total incompetence of civil laws in passing judgment on the Gospel of Christ and its interpretation. Thus this declaration reaffirms the complete independence of the Church from any government in fulfilling her task.*

This statement, resoundingly American in its essence, challenged especially European sensibilities, particularly those of bishops from countries having concordats with the Holy See, but in the end the vast majority substantially supported it as the mind of the Church.

Religious liberty and the rights of conscience were the Council subjects perhaps closest to Ritter's heart. The Fathers would debate these questions from November 18 to 21, 1963, but he advocated for this cause with American bishops even before the Fathers reassembled in Rome. Bishop Leo F. Dworschak of Fargo, North Dakota, contacted him in late February to promote the issue: "I am afraid that if the Bishops of the United States do not carry the ball on this play it will be fumbled. A failure at this point would be almost tantamount to a vindication of Father Feeney." Leonard Feeney was the Boston Jesuit whom Pope Pius XII excommunicated in 1948 because he insisted on a fundamentalist interpretation of *"Extra ecclesiam nulla salus"* ("Outside the Church there is no salvation"), in effect teaching that absolutely no one living outside the Roman Catholic Church could possibly be saved. Dworschak proposed to Ritter that the freedom of religion and rights of conscience should be the substance of the annual bishops' statement for 1963.

Partially in response to such suggestions, in his November 18 intervention Ritter also made a request that many others would echo before the Decree was finally promulgated: "Terminology which is perhaps offensive to our separated brethren should be removed in the emendations to be made by the Secretariat. Without a judgment about their Orders and Eucharistic celebrations, we strenuously ask that the term 'Church' not be denied these Christian groups which in the text are called 'communities.'"

In all of his interventions the cardinal had help from his *periti*—Monsignor Joseph Baker, Father Nicholas Persich, and, at times, Monsignor William Baum, *peritus* for Bishop Charles Helmsing of Kansas City-St. Joseph, Missouri, the chairman of the National Catholic Welfare Conference (NCWC) Office for Ecumenism, of which Baum was a staff member. But his words and actions were fundamentally his own; his decisions on matters in his own diocese often anticipated what the Council would later promulgate for the entire Church.

Cardinal Joseph Ritter (right) confers with Leo Jozef Cardinal Suenens, of Brussels, Belgium, in St. Peter's Basilica at Vatican II on December 2, 1963.

(AP WIREPHOTO)

In his last intervention on November 25, Cardinal Ritter closed with these words:

> *Finally, dear brothers, let me add a few words which do not especially apply to conciliar business. The sudden and violent death of our beloved John Fitzgerald Kennedy now moves the bishops of the United States of America to a very great sorrow. To you, brothers, we offer deep and sincere gratitude for all your expressions of condolence and promises of prayers. Where there is not charity and mutual consideration, hatred, whose fruit is death, easily seizes the heart of man. We pray and work in this Council so that we and our separated brethren may live together in the peace and charity of Christ always and that sometime in the future we may live in the same Christian unity.*

In an interview with Father Lawrence Landinik, O.F.M., an American Franciscan in Rome working on a doctorate in church history, Cardinal Ritter elaborated regarding ecumenism and religious liberty:

> *Remember, we're just making a beginning—we're just breaking ground ourselves in this matter of sincere, charitable dialogue. Ecumenism will be a long-range project and we don't know where it will lead. But at least it opens every good Christian's desire for union. Really, my experience in St. Louis has been of the tremendous desire of many Protestants for unity and a deep sorrow for the division.*

On the second topic:

> *By teaching this [religious liberty] the Council would be asserting man's right to freedom and happiness that comes from following one's conscience…As one cardinal told me: 'If you don't speak on this subject I lose my respect for you.'…One of the reasons why the Church in America is strong is because we have freedom, no interference from the State…Pius IX condemned religious liberty in a different context—the context of those who understood religious liberty as complete liberty from belief in God. As we are now understanding religious liberty, man*

is acting sincerely but always in relation to God…Our own Constitution tells us that our inalienable rights come from God. Otherwise, man depends on the State for his rights and he is subject to the State in everything…The Council's declaration on religious liberty must be seen in the light of man's dependence on God. For only when man depends on God is he truly free.

Religious Liberty

Religious liberty is a distinctively American contribution to politics and religion. When the thirteen colonies were being established, every country in Europe—except perhaps Holland—had a national church. Some were Catholic and some Protestant. Among the colonizers were Baptists and Quakers, both advocates of freedom of conscience. The colonies became the first place in the world where complete religious freedom was actually tried in a political state. Roger Williams incorporated the principle in his founding of Rhode Island in the 1640s.

By the end of the colonial period, a plurality of the population was unaffiliated with any church, and they were reluctant to grant special privileges to any one religious group. James Madison and Thomas Jefferson, two of the leaders of the movement to separate church and state in the establishment of independence, were strongly influenced by the Enlightenment and were not church members. It should not have been a surprise, then, that the American bishops at Vatican Council II would take the lead in promoting the cause of religious liberty.

9

The Second Vatican Council Years

Part Two (1964 and 1965)

Cardinal Ritter knew that there was strong resistance from many Council Fathers to the draft proposals on both ecumenism and religious liberty. It was very possible that neither would pass unless more support was generated for them. On January 27, 1964, he sent a "Confidential Memorandum" to some of the American bishops:

> *Your Excellency, I have been reliably informed that the Secretariat for the Promotion of Christian Unity has received a flood of emendations opposing the proposed texts of chapters of the schema on Ecumenism relating to Religious Liberty and the relationship between the Church and the Jews. At the same time almost no interventions have been received favoring the adoption of statements on these subjects preserving the spirit embodied in chapters IV and V of the draft.*
>
> *I am enclosing a copy of the written intervention I submitted to the Unity Secretariat on December 3, 1963, before leaving Rome. If you feel as I do that the adoption of meaningful declarations on these*

subjects is of great importance to the well-being of the Church, I would urge that you also send written observations to Cardinal Bea in his capacity as president of the Secretariat for the Promotion of Christian Unity. If possible, these observations should be in by January 31, 1964 [attached was Ritter's intervention in Latin].

On February 27 he wrote to Cardinal Cushing in Boston, urging him to send

...as soon as possible a personal letter in English to our Holy Father on behalf of a statement by the Council on both religious liberty and on the Jews...Please do not defer this but do it promptly. I am now working on a similar letter and Cardinal Meyer has written that he has already sent a personal plea to the Holy Father as also to the Secretariat for Christian Unity.

We must try to remove the misgivings of those in Rome and maybe the Holy Father himself about the reaction, political or otherwise, to such statements. We all should know how fatal it is for the Church not to speak out boldly, let the chips fall where they may, on the moral questions of the day. For instance, how sad it is today that the Church in the United States was silent so long on the Race question, and, right or wrong, the criticism of Pope Pius XII and the Bishops of Germany for failing to denounce Hitler and especially his insane and brutal massacre of the Jews.

The Church may suffer because of such courage but it will rebound to her credit in history and above all will bring a new confidence and loyalty to the Church among her own people and win the nations back to her leadership. You know how it would be a calamity for the Church if these subjects were by-passed by the Council or some mere gesture made in her behalf. In the eyes of the world the Council, no matter what else it did, would be a failure.

I am informed on rather good authority that the Holy Father wants this next session to be "resolutive," which would mean the close of the Council. So we must raise our voices now and effectively if we are not to be embarrassed and disappointed.

The tone of this letter as well as its contents reveal just how deeply Cardinal Ritter felt about ecumenism and religious liberty. The actions he had taken regarding these two concerns both at Indianapolis and in St. Louis arose not from some spontaneous, momentary sentiment but from convictions deeply imbedded in his mind and heart. He saw the Vatican Council as an opportunity to induce the whole Church to embrace a new direction on two crucial questions of the day. He would leave no stone unturned in working to achieve this goal.

Bishop Fulton Sheen on February 28 sent Ritter a copy of the letter he had sent to Cardinal Bea. In acknowledgment, the cardinal replied: "Sometimes I think we are too late but [let's] keep hoping and working just the same. It would be tragic if the Council failed to meet the world's expectations in these two fields." Five days later he thanked Bishop Hugh A. Donohue of Stockton, California, for the copy of his intervention that he had sent to the Secretariat. "A number of bishops have assured me of their interventions and I hope our voices will be heard. It is true what you say: The council will be judged by what it does with chapters four and five."

Bishops Robert Tracy of Baton Rouge, Louisiana, and Albert Fletcher of Little Rock, Arkansas, also sent the cardinal copies of the interventions they forwarded to Rome. Archbishop-Bishop John M. Gannon, of Erie, Pennsylvania, sent a copy of his intervention and accompanied it with a personal letter, which read, in part:

> In the great encyclical of Pope John, Pacem in Terris, the sentence that stood out most prominently and which received universal approval was: "Also among man's rights is that of being able to worship God in accordance with the right dictates of his own conscience, and to profess his religion both in private and in public." Never was more attention and favorable comment given to a Roman document as was given to this encyclical of Pope John....Our Lord intended to build His supernatural religion and revelation on this natural principle. He used human freedom as a foundation for the practices and obligations from which to build a supernatural life of Grace. The great revelation of our Lord was love, not authority.

Archbishop Karl J. Alter of Cincinnati contacted Ritter on March 19, asking that his *peritus*, Father Persich, be requested to prepare a "formal and well-organized statement of our position (on relations between the Church and State and on religious liberty) such as the Administrative Board of the NCWC might consider favorably and recommend perhaps to the rest of the Hierarchy of our country." He made the request because there would be no meeting of the bishops prior to the resumption of the Council in September and because he felt that the bishops of the United States should be of one mind on this subject.

Earlier in March, Archbishop Hallinan wrote to ask Ritter's permission to quote some of his words to the Council. Ritter cautioned that a direct quote could be considered a breach of confidence and violation of the Council's secrets. He continued: "You know, of course, that much of this material represents collaboration with my theologians and I might even say a great deal of it." He was not above giving credit where credit was due, and his two *periti*— Monsignor Joseph Baker and Father Nicholas Persich, C.M.—were bright, hard-working, and dedicated assistants who served him well with advice and moral support during the many months of the Council Sessions.

LIFE BACK IN ST. LOUIS

In the urgent work and conferring on Vatican Council matters, it's easy to forget that life in the archdiocese went on as usual, and the archbishop was an integral part of it. He perhaps felt something akin to a juggler, keeping an array of balls in the air simultaneously.

Believing that the benefits and responsibilities of citizenship must be available to all, Cardinal Ritter dispensed the Sisters of the Visitation—a cloistered order of nuns—so that they could leave their convent to vote in an important St. Louis County bond-issue election in April 1964. It was the first time since 1833 that the community of nuns was permitted to leave the convent, according to chancery office personnel.

The National Catholic Rural Life Conference (NCRLC) held its annual convention in St. Louis from August 27 to 30, 1964. The theme was "Accomplishments of the Past and Challenges of the Future." It was the fortieth anniversary of the conference, which had been founded in St. Louis

Gregory Cardinal Meyer (left) of Chicago and Joseph Cardinal Ritter talk before the opening of a working session of Vatican II on September 21, 1964.

(AP WIRE PHOTO)

in 1923. Cardinal Ritter played host, and Bishop John L. Morkovsky of Galveston-Houston, Texas, was president of the organization.

The opening day marked the eighty-third birthday of Monsignor George Hildner of St. Joseph Parish in Gildehaus, Missouri, who was affectionately known as "Alfalfa George" for his long years of dedication to improving the lot of farmers through promoting crop rotation; rural electrification; and advancements in farm implements, soil research, and seed quality. He was one of the few living charter members of the Conference, originally formed by eighty persons. He also served as the archdiocesan Rural Life Director. A nationally known conservationist, Monsignor Hildner helped organize the Missouri Association of Soil Conservation District Supervisors and served as its secretary-treasurer. On August 10, Pope Paul VI had named him a "Protonotary Apostolic," the highest title for a priest who is not a bishop.

He was invested with this new dignity during the convention's opening Solemn Pontifical Mass celebrated by Cardinal Ritter at the Cathedral. Pope Paul VI sent a greeting to the convention and noted: "We see so many poor suffering people who lack what is considered necessary for survival. Only recently nations have undertaken a cooperative program to provide food for the undernourished and developing nations. The United States with its vast resources has been in the forefront of this program, giving of its bounty to needy peoples."

Politics and pressure were never far from the center of activities at such conventions. The diocesan directors of the NCRLC voted to support the National Farmers' Organization in its plan to have farmers hold back from the market hogs, cattle, and sheep in an effort to improve prices.

THIRD SESSION OF VATICAN II

The Vatican Council convened its Third Session on September 14, 1964, the Feast of the Holy Cross. For the first time laywomen joined the laymen who were acting as "auditors" representing international Catholic organizations. On September 23, Bishop De Smedt of Belgium presented the text of the "Declaration on Religious Liberty." A vehement debate followed. Cardinal Ritter argued:

The declaration of human freedom itself and the arguments advanced on behalf of this freedom in the declaration should be considered separately. Religious freedom is a natural right of every man, only an aspect of natural human freedom, a certain truth, and only limited by the common good of society. The arguments for religious freedom in the schema do not enjoy the same simplicity, clarity, and certainty as the simple declaration of religious freedom itself. It would be better, therefore, to restrict the declaration to a simple affirmation and advocacy of religious liberty because the arguments in the schema lend themselves to interminable disputes about accidental points...with the danger that the Fathers, in rejecting the arguments, will also reject the declaration of religious freedom itself.

Not everyone was pleased with this intervention. Some thought he was conceding too much, especially after the campaign he had waged among the American bishops prior to the Session. Father Godfrey Diekmann, O.S.B., observed in a letter to his superior, Abbot Baldwin: "Ritter's intervention on Religious Liberty was disappointing." However, the cardinal recognized the strength of the opposition to the proposed decree and judged that a concession on some points would be the best way of ensuring that the declaration would receive final approval. Cardinal Koenig and Archbishop Parente also espoused this position.

Cardinal Bea presented to the Fathers the text on the so-called "Jewish Declaration" on September 25. Again acrimonious argumentation followed. On September 28, Cardinal Ritter spoke, focusing on paragraph 32:

The schema is most acceptable particularly in reparation for the injustices perpetrated against the Jews by Christians down through the centuries, even in documents and prayers.

1. The declaration should treat more fully and explicitly the religious patrimony which binds even today the Jewish people and Christians so closely together. Our relationship with the Jews, so hesitantly mentioned in the schema, should be proclaimed in a spirit of love and with great joy.

2. *Lines 23–27 concerning the conversion of the Jews should be transferred to the end of the declaration and should be made universal to embrace the conversion of all.*

3. *The final article in paragraph 32 should be removed. It confers nothing toward the correction of error for the reparation of injustices and, in fact, because it exonerates only Jews of our time, it doubles the injustice and error. A paragraph should be inserted with explicit mention of the Catechism of the Council of Trent which teaches that our sins are responsible for the death of Christ.*

Not all the Fathers would agree with those sentiments, but all had to admire the courage and forthrightness with which he stated them.

The "Decree on the Lay Apostolate" was debated for six days beginning on October 7. Cardinal Ritter was one of the first to speak, and he centered his remarks on three flaws that needed to be corrected:

…its clerical spirit, seen in its patronizing tone and in its placing the highest form of apostolate in aid to priests with hardly any acknowledgment of the nature and capabilities of the layman; its juridicism, found in the articles on the revision of Canon Law and their relation between hierarchy and laity—articles that don't even belong in a pastoral decree; and its favoritism of Catholic Action at the expense of other forms of the apostolate.

Cardinal Ritter's years of experience with apostolic groups such as the Legion of Mary and St. Vincent de Paul Society, as well as the Archdiocesan Councils of Catholic Men and Catholic Women, provided him with firsthand knowledge of how much the laity could contribute to the work of the Church if they were encouraged to do so. In many sectors of the worldwide Church the laity were still held captive to the old adage that they were there to "pay, pray, and obey."

On Friday, October 9, 1964, Pope Paul VI

yielded to political pressure outside and inside the Church and decided to block the declarations on the Jews and on religious freedom in the Council and submit them to bodies dominated by the Curia for further checking...Immediately we [Hans Kung and others] organize the resistance. On Saturday morning Bishop Elchinger mobilizes the French Cardinals Liénart and Joseph Lefèbvre (Bourges) and the American Cardinals Meyer and Ritter. I myself telephone Joseph Ratzinger in the Anima so that he can immediately put Cardinal Frings in the picture, and Karl Rahner, so that he can make contact with Cardinals Koenig and Döpfner. The Cardinals mentioned meet in the Anima as early as Sunday, [and] at the invitation of Cardinal Frings, Alfrink, Silva Henriquez and Léger are also here (Suenens in Belgium for the elections). They compose a letter of protest to the pope with the opening words "magno cum dolore"—"with great pain"; it finally goes to the pope with the signatures of thirteen cardinals. (Hans Kung, My Struggle for Freedom, *p. 421.*)

On October 20, the debate began on the Pastoral Constitution on the Church in the Modern World. Eight days later Cardinal Ritter offered his intervention. "The dignity of the human person and its recognition in practice is the necessary basis for all human life, whether individual or social." He insisted that the text be more emphatic in stating this. He then continued: "Such an acknowledgment can take root only in the mind and heart of each man." He spoke of the principles that would help underline this dignity: "...the practical recognition that each man's dignity requires his total dedication to the honor of God, and that each live in such a way that he manifest a concern for his intimate union with God." He concluded as follows:

Regrettably, Christians often substitute collective activity and responsibility for their own personal conscience: Too often it is rather the case that the world molds the Christian than that the Christian molds the world...By their silence, if not by their activity, they are guilty of infidelity towards God. The concepts of personal responsibility and rational obedience should be made clear in the schema so that all Christian faithful, aware of their relationship with God and of their worth, may show the world the transcendent value of human life and the true dignity of the human person.

On November 6, Pope Paul VI suddenly appeared in the assembly and opened discussion on the draft schema on the missions, urging its acceptance. Cardinal Agagianian offered some statistics:

In 1870 territories under the Propaganda Fidei still included England, Ireland, Holland, Luxembourg, North Germany, the United States and Canada. They were removed from the Propaganda in 1908. In 1870 there were 175 ecclesiastical jurisdictions in mission territories; today there are 770. In 1870 there was not one native Bishop in the mission territories, with the exception of Oriental Patriarchs and Prelates in the Far and Middle East. Today there are 41 Archbishops and 50 Bishops. At the time of Vatican I there were scarcely 10 seminaries for native clergy; today there are 385 minor and 81 major seminaries.

A major advancement had occurred in less than a century. The Church had expanded from a basically Western European entity to a truly "catholic" position in the world, spreading the Good News to peoples of many races, languages, and cultures. The Council Fathers had only to look around the *aula* of St. Peter's to see how true this was. But Cardinal Frings argued for a rejection of the draft in favor of one that would really come to grips with the challenges of the missions. His intervention carried the day. The schema as proposed was defeated and a new one called for. Pope Paul VI was disappointed and wept.

The Declaration on Christian Education was offered for debate on November 17 and Cardinal Ritter intervened that same day. He expressed his pleasure with the schema and then cited some points that "deserve special praise."

I am glad the schema encourages, in various ways, freedom within the educational field. However, in treating of the right of parents to freely select schools, the schema should also declare the right and obligation which parents have in school administration. In like manner the schema should more clearly and distinctly follow up those things which are mentioned in paragraph nine about the freedom of scientific inquiry. For if the Church teaches that truth is one, and if she believes that all truth leads to God, and if she professes that truth makes men free, then Catholic schools and universities should be examples of that true freedom which greatly benefits students and teachers.

In conclusion, I propose that the schema more explicitly and broadly consider the nature and limits of Catholic schools. Our schools are not established in order to separate Catholics from all others or to guard our boys and girls from the life outside; rather they are set up so that parents, priests, religious and lay Catholics, of their own free will and with great sacrifice, might better serve both God and mankind. For Catholic schools should be of great service for the communities in which they live and for human society itself. Otherwise, they would be unworthy of the name "Catholic schools."

Cardinal Ritter was almost uniquely qualified to speak on this subject. The Catholic schools program in St. Louis enjoyed the benefit of teaching personnel from numerous communities of religious men and women. Their predecessors had established headquarters in the city decades before, because it was truly the "Gateway to the West" for the Church as it spread from the Mississippi River to the Rocky Mountains. As these communities sent members westward, they also set up schools and other institutions at their base of operations, making St. Louis rich in educational facilities—from grade school through the university level. As a man fully committed to Catholic education, Ritter presided over an archdiocese whose people understood the value of a good Catholic education and were willing to sacrifice to maintain it. Many of the bishops who heard his remarks served dioceses with few if any Catholic schools and perhaps judged what he said to be unrealistic. But he spoke with a confidence founded upon personal experience.

On November 17, the revised text of the Declaration on Religious Liberty was also presented. It had been radically reworked. The next day Archbishop Felici, the General Secretary, announced that many Fathers had demanded a new debate on this radically changed text, and that the following day a preliminary vote would be taken to find whether the Fathers approved of the new text.

However, on November 19, Cardinal Tisserant, as dean of the Council presidency, announced that a vote would not be taken. An explosion of confusion and controversy erupted. For one *peritus* this day was the most exciting of the whole Council. Father Godfrey Diekmann wrote to his abbot:

> *Instantaneously some U.S. bishops left their seats. They gathered around Meyer and Ritter. Quinn, Reh, Unterkoefler channeled their anger into concrete action—circulated a petition and got over 800 signatures asking the Holy Father to assure that the Declaration would be brought to the floor for a vote before the end of the Session. (Bugnini telephoned—when I told him about Meyer and Ritter, et al, he said: "Bisogna combatte"—"they need to fight.") Proud that this was predominantly and overwhelmingly American. In some ways I'm glad it happened. Collegiality came into its own.*

The petition asked Pope Paul VI "urgently, more urgently, most urgently" to intervene and assure a vote on the religious liberty decree the following day, but the decision not to vote was upheld by the Pope in order to give the Fathers sufficient time to study it. He indicated that, if at all possible, it would be the first order of business at the Fourth Session, which would probably be called in the fall of 1965. Many of the proponents, including Cardinal Ritter, left Rome fearing that the Declaration might never see the light of day as a statement of what the Catholic Church believed about religious liberty as it should be understood in the twentieth century.

On the final working day of the Third Session, debate began on the marriage text. In his words to the Fathers, Cardinal Ritter proved to be somewhat of a prophet. He noted that he was "highly pleased" with the document, especially the provision dealing with mixed marriages. He singled out the proposed change in Church law, which at the time required both parties in mixed marriages to promise to baptize their children and rear and educate them as Catholics. The document proposed that only the Catholic party be required to make these promises. "Adoption of the suggested proposal would strengthen respect for divine law by stressing more emphatically the role of personal responsibility. Responsibility for the security of his own faith as well as for the Catholic education of their children is rightly placed upon the Catholic party. In this way we can lessen the possibility of offense to the consciences of our separated brethren."

Cardinal Ritter chatting with Sister Mary Luke, of Nerinx, Kentucky, the only American woman auditor at the Council, in October 1964.

He favored the proposal to authorize certain changes in the form of mixed marriages, which at the time could be contracted before a Catholic priest only and in the presence of Catholic witnesses. He said, "To demonstrate our respect for human dignity and to reduce the principles of ecumenism to practice, it is apparent that in some cases the ordinary must be empowered to grant a dispensation from the form."

Finally, he noted: "For the sake of honesty and justice those baptized in the Catholic Church who have been reared without a Catholic education must not be bound by the canonical form of marriage nor restricted by any impediments of merely ecclesiastical law." All of these were finally inserted in the revised Code of Canon Law in 1983. Ritter's sensitivity regarding ecumenism was consistent and appropriate, and he did not hesitate to inject it into Council discussions whenever he deemed it necessary. The auxiliary bishops of New York argued against his position at the urging of Cardinal Spellman and one hundred other bishops from the United States.

On the final day of the Third Session, November 21, 1964, the "Constitution on The Church," and the Decree on Ecumenism, together with a second decree "On Eastern Catholic Churches" were approved. The vote on the Ecumenism decree was 2,137 to 11.

When he returned to St. Louis, Cardinal Ritter expressed his disappointment at the blocking of the vote on religious liberty: "It would be impossible to measure the disappointment of the Council Fathers at the failure to record a preliminary vote on religious liberty. Our feeling of frustration at being bilked at the threshold of a first vote on the subject was heightened by the conviction that we were stalled by the delaying tactics of a very small minority." He went on to say, "His Holiness was very cordial and gracious. But he said he could not intercede on behalf of the vote on religious liberty. He said he did not believe he should inject himself into the action of the college of cardinals." The pope also told Cardinals Meyer of Chicago and Léger of Montreal that "the delay would give the chance to formulate a stronger religious liberty document with no theological faults."

William Woo of the *St. Louis Post-Dispatch* interviewed the cardinal after his return home and described him as follows:

Cardinal Ritter is 72 years old. He is a small man with gray eyes and thinning gray hair, and he spoke in a warm and undramatic manner that brought to mind a kindly priest rather than a prince of the Church....The office reflects the contemporary nature of the Chancery building, but is not severely modern. It is carpeted in beige and parts of the wall are paneled in cherry to match the desk. The decorations, too, are modest: a portrait of the Pope, a view of Coblenz, a vase of yellow chrysanthemums, a potted plant. On a wall behind his desk was a carved crucifix, and through the thin white curtains one could see to the east the green dome and gray stone of the Cathedral of St. Louis.

The Declaration on Religious Liberty was never far from Ritter's mind. On December 19, he wrote a letter to an unspecified number of bishops regarding the schema:

Your Excellency, As you are well aware, the Holy Father has assured us that the schema on religious liberty will be on the agenda for the Fourth and Final Session of the Council. However, since there has never been a preliminary vote on the subject, no text can be said to be "in possession." It is on this account that a number of bishops have urged me to write to solicit the support of the American hierarchy to maintain the text distributed just prior to the conclusion of the Third Session as the basis for discussion. If you are in accord with this proposal, I...suggest that you write to the Secretariat for Promoting Christian Unity (Via dei Corridori, 64, Rome) in this vein, adding any suggestions you may have for the further improvement of the declaration. Among my own recommendations for emendations of the text are these:

1. *The historical portion of the introduction (#2) should be revised and corrected. Herein the onus for religious intolerance is placed solely on civil authorities whereas it must be admitted that Christian Communions have most frequently been responsible for the strictures of the confessions' state.*

> *2. In part II (#4c) the description of the nature of religion seems somewhat Pelagian particularly when it speaks of "man ordaining himself directly to God."*

> *3. In part VI (#13) the text enters gratuitously into a theological controversy over the precise extent of the Church's authority in teaching the natural law.*

> *Permit me to emphasize the fact that these observations in no way mitigate the primary purpose in writing, which is to request retention of the present text as the basis for conciliar declarations. It is important to remember that all recommendations must be submitted prior to January 31, 1965.*

The carefulness with which Ritter composed this letter and the extent to which he went to delineate deficiencies in the text indicate his concern for the eventual disposition of the declaration and the whole issue of religious liberty. Continuing the battle to keep it alive in the face of determined opposition in the Council showed again how crucial to him was this matter and how the Church would address it. He labored almost to the point of exhaustion to make sure he had done all within his power to bring about the proper outcome.

The day-to-day care of the St. Louis Archdiocese was maintained in the months intervening between the third and fourth sessions of the Council. However, it is of course to be expected that Cardinal Ritter's attention was somewhat split between the archdiocese and preparation for the final session.

On August 9, 1965, in a letter to Lawrence Cardinal Shehan of Baltimore, congratulating him on his appointment to "the presidency of the Council and also to the Holy Office," Ritter wrote: "I am writing, however, to express my hope that you will not fail to send in an intervention on religious liberty before the deadline. September 8th, I believe. I have been assured Cardinal Spellman will speak and I am sure Cardinal Cushing, too. You will now be in a strategic position and I know you will make the most of it, especially on this important matter for the Church of the United States."

Cardinal Ritter visited children at a Christmas party held at Rosati-Kain High School on December 23, 1964.

FOURTH COUNCIL SESSION

The Fourth Session of the Council was convened on September 14, 1965. Pope Paul VI in his speech expressed his concern about the Council's problems, which he believed could only be solved by love. "A person only really knows a thing if he loves it."

One last time Cardinal Ritter spoke in the Council on the subject of religious liberty. On September 16 he praised the Secretariat for their work in producing a

> *...strong, clear, and precise affirmation of religious liberty...The whole world is watching Rome and awaits a document which brings joy to the hearts of very many and eases their lives..."The love of Christ urges us" to approve the document which has already been accepted... Justice demands that we present men with the Declaration on Religious Liberty in a thorough presentation. For in some Catholic countries, our brothers in Christ—separated, but still our brothers—suffer many things because of sincere and even Christian consciences. At least some of these religious persecutions had their origin in ecclesiastical regulations. Should we not repair these unjust conditions which result from our doing?...Finally, unless we shall have approved a firm and clear Declaration on Religious Liberty, many things in the conciliar Constitution on the Church and in the Decree on Ecumenism, which have already been promulgated, will remain without meaning, value or truth....Let us approve this Declaration on Religious Liberty lest we deserve by our negligence to be counted among the enemies of the Gospel.*

On September 22, the declaration was accepted, 1,997 to 224. This paved the way for the final vote for promulgation by the pope and bishops on December 7: 2,308 yes, 70 no, 8 null. The Declaration on Religious Liberty became one of the sixteen documents of Vatican Council II.

The Declaration was the distinctive American contribution to Vatican II. Father John Courtney Murray, S.J., who contributed so much to the thinking that went into the document, said, "The achievement of the Declaration on Religious Liberty was to bring the Church, at long last, abreast of the consciousness of civilized mankind, which has already accepted religious freedom as a principle and as a legal institution."

No one appreciated this more than Cardinal Ritter. He worked tirelessly between Sessions to promote its acceptance and advocacy among the American bishops. He spoke ardently on this subject in his conciliar interventions. When it seemed doomed, shunted aside at the end of the Third Session, he joined other leaders in appealing to the pope to keep it from succumbing to the machinations of opponents, both within and without the Council chamber. His dedication to this cause came from his profound conviction that religious liberty is a God-given right that must be respected and cannot be denied. To nothing in his life did he devote more energy and commitment.

As he sailed home on the *S.S. Constitution*, he released a press statement on December 22, 1965:

> *The scope of the Council has ranged from a studied re-examination of the Church and her worship, to an affirmation of the principle of religious liberty and carefully considered guidelines for the future relationship of the Church and Catholics with other Christians and non-Christians. The note of Christian service has been stressed particularly in the consideration of the problems of our present age…The impact of Vatican II has been increased by the…media, which have told its story to the world with utmost candor and fairness…With God's help the Catholic Church in St. Louis and its archbishop will extend every effort to make the Christian renewal of Vatican II a living reality.*

The Council issued a total of sixteen documents: four constitutions on the liturgy, the Church's structure and nature, the Church in the modern world, and on Divine revelation; nine decrees: on the Church and the media, ecumenism, Eastern Catholic churches, bishops, priestly formation, religious life, the laity, priestly ministry, and missionary activity; and three declarations: on non-Christian religions, Christian education, and religious liberty.

The opening of the Fourth Session of Vatican II in St. Peter's Basilica. Next to Cardinal Ritter of St. Louis (holding book) is Laurean Cardinal Rugambwa of Tanganyika.

10

Post–Vatican II Years
(1966 and 1967)

On January 7, 1966, the City of St. Louis, in recognition of Ritter's return after Vatican II, extended "the warm gratitude of the people of St. Louis for the honor and distinction which has been brought to our beloved St. Louis by the strength, wisdom, courage and humor of our great Cardinal, and does, by these presents, extend our congratulations and affection to Cardinal Ritter of St. Louis."

One reporter described him as "a small man with a generous manner and an underlying streak of iron." A close associate sketched him as "a basically humble man who doesn't go for all the fuss and feathers." At one banquet attended by members of the local professional baseball and football teams, he quipped that he was the "only Cardinal not sponsored by a brewery."

On March 3, Bishop Paul F. Tanner, General Secretary of the National Catholic Welfare Conference (later renamed the United States Conference of Catholic Bishops), requested input from Ritter on the follow-up November statement after the fall meeting of the U.S. bishops. Eight days later the cardinal replied, "My first thought regarding a suitable topic…is something pertaining to the Vatican Council. It is highly desirable to keep the spirit of the Council in the minds of the faithful. If the Council is to bear lasting fruit it must firmly take hold in the lives of us all. I feel that an exhortation from the Bishops on this subject would be quite timely."

On March 7, Ritter wrote to William Cardinal Conway of Armagh, Ireland, "I see from the papers the implementation of the Council decrees grows apace in the land of saints and scholars. Your Eminence is specifically mentioned along with many of their Excellencies. What impressed me was the readiness of the people to implement. We are having programs in individual dioceses but I am afraid we are lagging on the national level. Our clergy and people are also very eager to get going."

Not only was he eager to see the Council take hold in the United States; he was equally avid in offering encouragement to those in Rome responsible for carrying out the postconciliar projects that flowed directly from Council decisions. On June 13 he wrote to Augustine Cardinal Bea:

> *Your Eminence: I am writing to express my satisfaction and support for the Directory on Ecumenism prepared by the Secretariat for Promoting Christian Unity. I am very much in agreement with the decision not to attempt a detailed directory covering every aspect of the Ecumenical Movement at this time. It is evident that insights gained by experience will assist in the evolution of ecumenical practice.*
>
> *I am particularly pleased with the section treating of baptism, and the observations on the practice of conditional baptism. I believe that, in concert with the Post Conciliar Commission on Sacred Liturgy, it might be possible to draw up such a rite which might entail the renewal of baptismal vows, a profession of faith in a short form, and the bestowal of the kiss of peace by the priest and representatives of the congregation as a sign of reception into full ecclesiastical communion. Such a rite might well take place within the celebration of Holy Mass.*
>
> *It might be harmful for good ecumenical relations in the United States and other parts of the world in which there are large numbers of Protestants to emphasize unduly our regard for the Orthodox churches. Too great a distinction in our approach to the Orthodox and to the Protestant churches might well lead us into an unrealistic anticipation of union with the Orthodox while overlooking the fact that the attitude and spirit of many Protestant churches support a more genuine foundation for ecumenical hope.*

As a member of the Post-Conciliar Commission on Sacred Liturgy, Cardinal Ritter was aware of plans to renew the rites of baptism and saw a potential linking of the Secretariat with that Commission in revising those rites that would be advantageous to the work of both groups. He also knew from his experience that at that time the Protestant churches in St. Louis were more favorable to ecumenical overtures than were the Orthodox. But Bea was hearing from others with a different view, which the Secretariat also had to consider.

Ritter's liturgical expertise attracted people seeking his advice. On August 24, Reverend Thomas O'Day, S.J., wrote to ask the cardinal for comments on O'Day's proposed new prayer leaflet for the "Apostles of Prayer" movement in New York. Ritter answered the next day, giving his approval for the changes and commenting: "It meets the trend of updating and modernizing going on in all venues of life including the Church. I am sure it will please everyone and its attractiveness makes for easier reading."

One of the challenges facing dioceses after Vatican II was how to get its message to the faithful in ways that would be both instructive and engaging. St. Louis answered the challenge by developing "Operation Renewal," an archdiocesan-wide program consisting of 2,600 parish study groups that met to discuss the Council documents in a digested form, more easily presented with appropriate questions to stimulate discussion. People were eager to engage in this process and it was very popular at the parish level. The goal of the enterprise was an archdiocesan "Little Council," convened when the discussion phase was complete and the resulting recommendations had been digested and formulated for voting. Cardinal Ritter's untimely death short-circuited the program in mid-course, and it never regained the momentum it had enjoyed at its beginning in 1966.

That same fall, at the annual meeting of the 3,000 religious and lay teachers in the archdiocesan school system, Cardinal Ritter gave an address, parts of which were quoted in the daily newspapers. On November 30, J. Blaine Fister, of the National Council of the Churches of Christ, wrote to the cardinal:

> You were quoted as saying that the public schools should not remain *"silent"* on the subject of religion. And you further went on to say that *"the new spirit of cooperation among churches"* and the recent U.S.

Supreme Court decisions should open the way for the public school system to review their attitude toward religion in the schools. This is very much in keeping with what our position in the National Council of Churches has been regarding this issue.

Cardinal Ritter went to Rome again for the plenary session of the Post-Conciliar Commission for the Liturgy, which took place from October 6 to 20. Meanwhile, back at home there was unrest due to actions he had taken regarding four of his priests. The "Letters from the People" in the *St. Louis Post-Dispatch* of November 29 carried several from people of the archdiocese expressing their disappointment over the transfers of the priests: Fathers Raymond Rustige, Francis Matthews, David Thomas, and John Daly. Two other priests—Fathers Michael Cleary and William Lally—also wrote the newspaper saying that they were "hurt by their transfers from these positions (on matters of controversy), because we feel they represented freedom of thought and speech of the Catholics of this archdiocese."

A group of priests, religious, and laity had been meeting to discuss the documents of Vatican II in their original form to discern how they could be implemented on the local level. They concluded that the priests in question had been removed from their assignments in June, the time of the year when assignments were usually made, because they had disagreed with the pace of renewal in the archdiocese. Father Rustige had been associate editor of the *St. Louis Review;* Father Matthews was director of the Archdiocesan News Bureau and of the Archdiocesan Radio and Television Apostolate; Father Thomas, executive secretary of the Archdiocesan Commissions on Sacred Liturgy, Sacred Music and Sacred Art, and assistant to the chancellor; and Father Daly was Father Matthews' assistant. Fathers Rustige and Matthews became pastors; Father Thomas, the chaplain of the Sisters of the Most Precious Blood in O'Fallon, Missouri; Father Daly, an assistant pastor. At the same time came an elimination of the publication for priests, titled "Inter Nos," which afforded those who wished an avenue for expressing their interests and concerns to fellow members of the archdiocesan priesthood.

Later the cardinal sent a letter to his priests threatening to reassign any priests who experimented with the liturgy without permission. Specifically mentioned in the letter as being forbidden were the use of English in the Canon of the Mass, additions or omissions of words and gestures, "the indiscriminate distribution of Holy Communion under both species," and the celebration of Mass outside a church or chapel without permission. This letter was occasioned in part by the "Christian Experiment," an informal group of 125 people who had been experimenting with the liturgy in St. Louis.

Meanwhile Cardinal Ritter was proceeding with his own plan for implementing the directives of Vatican II beyond the program "Operation Renewal." In his Christmas pastoral letter he wrote: "The Vatican Council, whose first anniversary we are commemorating, has now set us on a new course of Christian living, one which more properly conforms to Christ's life, one which makes us conscious of being the Christs of our day, proclaiming by our lives and our efforts the good news of salvation." On December 27 he disclosed plans to create a twenty-member Council of Priests. He entered DePaul Hospital on December 29 for his annual three-day checkup.

On January 6, 1967, the cardinal answered a letter sent to him by the Very Reverend Paul Reinert, S.J., President of Saint Louis University, informing him of a major change planned for the makeup of the Board of Trustees.

> *I wish to acknowledge your kind letter of December 29, 1966, together with the resolution and time schedule endorsed by the University Trustees on December 21. My congratulations go to you and those who are working with you on the project for the enlargement of the Board of Trustees. It is a fine plan which will mean much for the University and the whole community it serves.*
>
> *Be assured of my enthusiasm and wholehearted support and approval of this proposal to enlarge your Board and involve laymen in the direction and policy-making responsibilities of the University. It is very much in keeping with the spirit of Vatican II.*

The university's action was bold for the time—placing laymen on the Board of Trustees, which until that time had been composed solely of Jesuits. Reinert solicited Ritter's support for the change with the expectation that having received it, some of the criticism aimed against the move would be averted.

On January 10 the archdiocese announced a new program entitled "Tithing for the Poor." Parishes were invited to conduct monthly collections, the proceeds to be forwarded to the chancery office, which would then use the money as grants-of-aid to inner-city and rural parishes in need of assistance. Another purpose of the program was to connect well-to-do parishes with those that were struggling because of meager financial resources or a scarcity of members with professional training. "Tithing for the Poor" was successful because it brought people into direct contact with each other, and the money generated was passed on directly to those in need without the expense of a bureaucratic level functioning between donors and recipients.

On February 7, Cardinal Ritter announced the appointment of an Archdiocesan Pastoral Council of twenty-two members composed of pastors, diocesan officials, religious, and laity. They would meet on a regular basis and serve in an advisory capacity regarding all matters concerning the apostolic work of the archdiocese. The first meeting of the Pastoral Council was scheduled for that spring.

That same day the cardinal replied to a letter from "Bud" alluding to his marriage to "Peg," which had been witnessed by Ritter thirty-five years earlier. A picture had accompanied the letter.

> *There is one more memory that I would mention which your picture in* The Criterion *recalled: The memory of my own happy years in Indianapolis. If I had not been under obedience to the Pope it would seem that I had abandoned my friends in Indianapolis when I left for St. Louis. When I look back on the occasion and recall the evidence I gave of reluctance to leave Indianapolis, I am surprised that St. Louis took me. A newspaper man associated earlier with one of the Indianapolis papers sent a word of consolation—"St. Louis is just like Indianapolis, only a little bigger." I have found this to be true and in these twenty years I feel that I have never left Indianapolis. I still treasure the memory of you good people and at the same time have found the people of St. Louis just like those of Indianapolis. I could pay no higher compliment to St. Louis. God gives us all a chance to find happiness in providing it by our service to others.*

This was almost a recapitulation of his whole life as priest, bishop, archbishop, and cardinal.

RESIGNATION AND GOLDEN JUBILEE

In the spring of 1967, Cardinal Ritter sent his resignation to the Vatican through the Apostolic Delegate, Archbishop Egidio Vagnozzi. It included a resolute request that it be accepted. The retirement age of seventy-five was set by Pope Paul VI in a decree issued in August of 1966: "All bishops...are earnestly encouraged of their own free will to tender their resignation from office not later than at the completion of their 75th year of age, to the competent authority which will make provision after examining all circumstances of individual cases" (*Motu Proprio "Ecclesiae Sanctae"*). In his letter, Ritter hinted that he would like to be a pastor in a country parish.

When the time came for him to celebrate his fiftieth anniversary as a priest, an associate suggested a testimonial dinner for civic leaders. The cardinal refused, noting that it was not an anniversary of the archdiocese, but simply a personal observance. It was then suggested that there be a Mass at the Cathedral to which everyone would be invited. He assented to that, but when it was further suggested that it should be a solemn Pontifical Mass, to which he as a prince of the Church was entitled, he declined. "I'll have a Mass, but it will be a very low Mass." It took place on April 30, a month ahead of the actual ordination date because he planned to celebrate May 30 with classmates in Indiana. Cardinal Ritter preached. A luncheon followed at the Chase Park Plaza Hotel. Father Paul Reinert, S.J., was the only speaker. Prior to that day he had sent a check for $5,000 from the Jesuit Community to the archdiocese in honor of the cardinal.

Acknowledgments of the jubilee came from a number of quarters:

+ Leo Cardinal Suenens of Belgium, with whom Ritter had worked so closely on a number at issues at Vatican II, sent his congratulations. In response, the jubilarian wrote: "These years have been years of great events for the Church and it has been an inspiring time to exercise the office of priesthood. I shall always sing the praises of the Lord for His mercy."

+ Representative Thomas Curtis of Missouri wrote from the House of Representatives in Washington on May 1: "If 'faith without works is dead' [then] you have demonstrated the converse for truly the vitality and vibrancy of your own commitment and the results of your witness are seen in the strength of the Catholic communion in our midst and the reputation of brotherhood and humanitarianism which you hold both here and abroad."

+ Thomas H. Gibbons, Jr., Director of Equal Employment Services, sent this note on May 7: "Almost two years ago Father Doyle brought me to your office to introduce me after we had launched Project Equality in the Archdiocese of St. Louis. This was the first Project Equality program in the country. As you know, there are now eighty-three participants and ten offices engaged in promoting equal employment opportunity both in church hiring and through church purchasing."

+ Perhaps the most significant of the messages Cardinal Ritter received came from Allen O. Miller, a theologian at Eden Theological Seminary, dated April 30: "We are so deeply appreciative of the fine ecumenical climate that now exists between us here in the St. Louis area and are more than thankful for your warmth and generous understanding that has caused this to be so....I have been honored and pleased to be asked to speak at so many Catholic institutions in the diocese. This is truly a great day to be alive."

In connection with his anniversary, the cardinal was interviewed on April 25 by Max Roby of television station KMOX-TV. He touched on a large number of topics, one of which was his retirement:

I said to someone recently that I think it is about time, perhaps, that I be asking to let some younger people take over and he said, "No, you have plenty mileage left." But I don't know how much mileage I have left...In all professions and all the various vocations...we know after a certain age that you are supposed to step aside for the young fellow and maybe that ought to be true in the Church, too. It is true. The council...indicated that bishops should think about giving up when they are seventy-five, at least at that time.

On Catholic schools, he commented:

When we come to the place where we find we cannot meet the demand and we cannot maintain good schools…we are going to ask the state to help us out, to take over these children in the public schools. If we were confronted with the question of whether we should start parochial schools today, I am sure they wouldn't be started. I think that if the bishops of the United States were confronted with our problem today, they would think a long time before they would allow the directive of the bishops of the Council of Baltimore over a hundred years ago directing pastors and directing the people to establish schools in every parish of the country.

His thoughts on Catholic schools were a significant step back from the total commitment to a diocesan Catholic school system he advocated and promoted in his early years in St. Louis. But the times had changed: staffing schools with religious had become much more difficult as the numbers of young women and men entering religious communities decreased and members left to return to the secular world, the cost of parochial education increasing as lay teachers replaced them. Such a change had not been envisioned by the bishops of the nineteenth century who were faced with huge numbers of immigrants seeking to retain their Catholic identity by close association with their parish community and school conducted by religious sisters and brothers with vows of poverty, chastity, and obedience, and dedicated to providing a sound education for their Catholic students.

To celebrate Ritter's fiftieth anniversary the archdiocese decided to dedicate the 1967 Expansion Fund as the "Golden Jubilee Fund Drive," with the general campaign to begin on Sunday, May 7. The letter from Auxiliary Bishop Glennon P. Flavin announcing the drive noted that the cardinal had built eleven high schools and started fifty-nine parishes. The theme for the drive was, "As You Appreciate So Shall You Give." In the brochure promoting the drive the cardinal wrote, "My greatest joy in this Golden Jubilee of my Priesthood would be your devotion to the Blessed Lord and Holy Church expressed in a truly sacrificial gift to our continuing Expansion Fund."

Plans for the future included a new coeducational high school in

Manchester for 1,000 students and a new Little Sisters of the Poor facility for 250 residents to be built in the city at 3225 North Florissant for occupancy by 1969, the centennial of their service in St. Louis. Especially featured in the brochure was the Urban Apostolate. More than 100,000 poor and unfortunate people were helped by this program in 1966, which involved eighteen parishes providing adult education, home improvement, leadership, preschool teaching, and teenage athletics to those in need.

A Final Vacation

In early May, Cardinal Ritter took a vacation in Hawaii. After arriving back home he sent a number of thank-you notes, all dated May 16:

- To Very Reverend John H. Joyce, M.M.: "The spirit of Hawaii is still on me and I find it hard to get back to work. I shall always be grateful for your hospitality and for all the fine arrangements you made to make our stay a pleasant one. I especially want to thank the Seminary or whoever was responsible for making up the Mass kit and if anything has been damaged in carrying it to and fro please let me know. I do not have too many years ahead for restitution."

- To Reverend Cyril Gombold, M.M.: "I am still under the spell of Hawaii and also of your fine inspiration during the days you were so generous in taking us around the island. It was a very enjoyable experience and surely a great contrast to Honolulu. On our way home I tried my best to get [Father John] Martin to believe in the Minnehunnes [sic] (watchful spirits hovering over the islands) but did not succeed. I know though, that they are always going to look after their friend and defender as well as their advocate."

Father John Martin, M.M., who accompanied the cardinal, was the superior of the house of studies the Maryknoll Fathers maintained in St. Louis on West Pine near the Cathedral. Over the years, the cardinal would visit there from time to time and Father Martin had become a close friend.

Cardinal Ritter celebrated his fiftieth ordination anniversary with two classmates—Monsignor Clement Bosler and Reverend Carl Riebenthaler—at

Millhouse, Indiana, on June 1, a date set at their request. May 30, the actual ordination date, was avoided because some of the priests wanted to attend the Indianapolis 500 race, and the roads "would be crowded with speeding drunk drivers for the return trip in the afternoon."

Bosler, Riebenthaler, and Ritter had been in the five-member graduating class at Saint Mary's parish school in New Albany. Bosler remembered Ritter as "a good student, very methodical, who had a burning ambition to be up and first in our dormitory [at St. Meinrad Seminary] in the morning. He was a very down-to-earth person, warm-hearted, a reliable friend and very democratic."

Most Reverend Angelo Dell'Acqua sent a message of congratulations from Vatican City. In reply, Ritter wrote: "The fifty years have been happy years and I have enjoyed work as a parish priest and as bishop. I think these past twenty-three [sic] years in St. Louis have been for me the happiest. It is difficult to work in one's home diocese which was the case when I succeeded Bishop Chartrand in Indianapolis."

Back home, the cardinal took up his usual schedule of activities. On June 2 he had lunch, as was his Friday custom, with a small group of diocesan priests. In his interview with Max Roby he had observed: "The priest of today is being challenged more than ever because of the development that has gone on in the world. In the field of education, for instance, the priest is dealing with a different kind of world than he did fifty years ago. So the preparation for the young man for the priesthood must be updated to meet the times in which we are living."

On June 3 he went to Kiel Auditorium for the commencement exercises of Saint Louis University and was asked to say a few words. He did so but declined the invitation to join the graduates at the luncheon following the ceremony. Eating with them would have been his last public act.

11

The Final Days

Cardinal Ritter had a heart attack on June 5, 1967, and was taken to DePaul Hospital. It was his first serious illness. The next day Monsignor William Drumm, the chancellor, wrote to Father John J. McCrystal of Fort Thomas, Kentucky, who had invited the cardinal to preach at his jubilee. "It seems that the Cardinal's physician wants him to rest up in the hospital and I am sure he will not be permitted to travel for a while. We do not think it is anything serious but the doctor wants to be on the safe side."

On June 8, Drumm wrote to Cardinal Spellman regarding a request he had made in soliciting a gift for the Apostolic Delegate, Egidio Vagnozzi, recently named to become a cardinal, to be given to him prior to the June 26 Consistory. "From his sick bed in DePaul Hospital His Eminence, our Cardinal, asked me to acknowledge your kind letter of June 1st, 1967, and to enclose this check for the Cardinal Vagnozzi Fund. At the same time His Eminence asked me to inform you of his condition which has, as you know, worsened since then."

Cardinal Ritter died at 5:47 AM on Saturday, June 10, 1967. Doctor Christopher G. Vournas, his physician, said, "His heart just failed from the strain." He received the Last Rites when he entered the hospital on Monday. Vigil had been kept since Wednesday by chancery officials and members of the Ritter family, including his sister, Sister Marie Catherine, who came from Bardstown, Kentucky, to be with him.

The funeral Mass took place on Thursday, June 15, at the Cathedral. Cardinal-designate John Cody, formerly an auxiliary bishop under Cardinal Ritter in St. Louis, was the main celebrant. Cardinals Cushing, McIntyre, Shehan, and Spellman attended, together with cardinal-designates Krol and O'Boyle. Ten archbishops, forty-eight bishops, and four abbots joined them. Some fifty Protestant, Jewish, and Orthodox leaders were present, representing the Episcopal Church, Missouri-Synod Lutheran, United Church of Christ, Greek Orthodox, Baptist, Disciples of Christ, Methodists, Presbyterians, and Salvation Army. In his sermon Bishop Charles Helmsing, another former auxiliary bishop under the cardinal, singled out his liturgical leadership, particularly "his concern for a liturgy of the Word that would truly inform and enlighten the people of God." White vestments, the selection of readings, and use of psalms gave evidence of the experimental funeral liturgy authorized in St. Louis by the Vatican since September 1966. Cardinal Ritter was buried in the priests' lot at Calvary Cemetery among some 200 graves. He had expressed the desire not to be buried in the Cathedral. Later his red hat was hung from the ceiling there to perpetuate his memory.

Present at Cardinal Ritter's funeral Mass at the New Cathedral were (left to right) Bishops Gottwald, Marling, Flavin, and Strecker. (The bishop second from right is unidentified.)

Also in attendance at Cardinal Ritter's funeral were (left to right) Cardinals Spellman, McIntyre, Cushing, and Shehan.

As one might expect, the tributes to a great man were many:

+ Governor Hearnes of Missouri commented: "Through more than 70 years of life and a half-century since he was ordained a priest, Cardinal Ritter demonstrated a humanitarian and religious application of his understanding and compassion for all men. His service was more than that of a citizen of Missouri during the 21 years since he became archbishop of St. Louis. His intelligence and ability made him a true citizen of the world."

+ Senator Edward V. Long, Democrat from Missouri, issued a statement in Washington: "He was a great American. His efforts for two decades in St. Louis and his 50 years as a priest have brought tremendous social progress for the peoples of our state and nation."

+ In an editorial in the *St. Louis Review* of June 16, the writer said: "The Cardinal was an able and gifted administrator, because he was able to delegate authority...To give but one instance, we cite the unlimited editorial freedom given to the *St. Louis Review* to exercise its function as a newspaper."

+ A Mass for the deceased cardinal was offered at St. Francis Xavier Church in Corozal Town, British Honduras, concelebrated by priests to whom Ritter had awarded scholarships for Kenrick Seminary: Fathers Harry Martin, Herbert Panton, Osmond Martin, Rene Gomez and Martin Avila. They sent the St. Louis chancery a picture of the occasion.

+ Father Frederick McManus, a *peritus* at Vatican Council II who worked closely with Cardinal Ritter on liturgical matters, recalled, "In the Council he spoke consistently and effectively for the progress that prevailed, for Episcopal collegiality and responsibility. To take one example, he offered the formulation which guarantees the bishop's pastoral office; instead of awaiting faculties and dispensations from the Pope, the bishop has his own pastoral responsibility fully recognized unless the Pope reserves a decision to himself. Thus a law was changed, and more important, a whole attitude and approach changed.

"Few bishops reared in another generation and other ways have grasped and welcomed the renewal as has the great Cardinal. A strong spokesman in the Council, he has been above all else open and willing, with a spirit much younger bishops and priests can emulate. A kind of supernatural instinct made him ready to accept change and also initiate it—a part of the true role of the bishop in the Church."

Cardinal Ritter's will was dated November 26, 1956. It assigned his property and that which he administered as head of the archdiocese to Bishop John Cody of Kansas City-St. Joseph, and Bishops-designate Charles Helmsing of Springfield-Cape Girardeau and Joseph Marling of Jefferson City (these were their titles in 1956), to be held by them in trust as joint tenants until a new archbishop was appointed. He appointed as executor of the will the person who would be serving as chancellor of the archdiocese at the time of his death. The will was filed at the Probate Court of St. Louis on June 12, 1967.

While an archbishop, Ritter consecrated eight bishops: Mark K. Carroll, John P. Cody, Leo J. Steck, Charles H. Helmsing, Leo C. Byrne, Glennon P. Flavin, David H. Hickey, S.J., and George J. Gottwald.

POSTSCRIPT

On November 2, 1994, Cardinal Ritter's remains were brought from Calvary Cemetery to the Cathedral. The re-interment in the crypt took place as part of the annual Mass for departed members of the Priests' Purgatorial Society. Monsignors Elmer Behrmann, Rowland Gannon, Bernard Granich and James Hartnett served as honorary pallbearers. Family members attending were Dr. Frank and Mrs. Trudy Ritter and their three children; Mrs. Shirley Ritter Edwards of Miami, Florida; Sister Francis Louise Ritter of Nerinx, Kentucky; Helen L. Ritter of Louisville, Kentucky; Dr. Frank Kraft and Mrs. Dolores Ritter of Port Clinton, Ohio; and Mr. George Gates and Mrs. Joann Ritter-Gates.

The cardinal's remains were laid to rest with those of John Joseph Cardinal Glennon and Archbishop John Lawrence May in the New Cathedral (now the Cathedral Basilica of St. Louis).

Epilogue

Cardinal Ritter served as the Archbishop of St. Louis for almost twenty-one years. Only Peter Richard Kenrick (1843–1895) and John Joseph Glennon (1903–1946) had longer tenures. The other ordinaries of St. Louis had varying lengths of service: Joseph Rosati, C.M. (1826–1843), John Kain (1895–1903), John Joseph Carberry (1968–1979), John May (1980–1992), and Justin Rigali (1994–2003).

Cardinal Ritter's episcopal career had two distinct periods: the thirteen years he worked in Indianapolis (1933–1946) and the years he spent in St. Louis (1946–1967). American life during these two eras, comparatively, was extraordinarily dissimilar. In the earlier years, people struggled with the Depression brought on by a collapsed economy, followed by a devastating World War. All they could do was to keep their lives together and deal with each day as it came along. Survival was the goal, whether in the neighborhoods of Middle America or on the battlefields of Europe and Africa and Asia and the Far East.

When the war ended in 1945 and the combatants came home, a new energy enveloped the country: the economy soared, jobs were created to respond to the demand for goods and services, babies were born, and America came alive, all set in motion by "the greatest generation."

Cardinal Ritter was uniquely qualified to lead the Catholics of St. Louis at that time of change. His experience as an assistant priest, rector of a cathedral, auxiliary bishop, administrator of a diocese, financial affairs manager, social justice advocate, and lay apostolate animator equipped him to face the challenges before him. Add to that his down-to-earth personality, his ability to ascertain the heart of a problem and central point of an issue, and his dogged determination to see a thing through once he decided it was important, and it seems clear that the Holy Spirit chose the right man to follow his beloved predecessor, Cardinal Glennon.

At the time of his death the population of the St. Louis Archdiocese was 1,768,468, of whom 512,152 were Catholic. There were 260 parishes and missions, which, together with the many schools, hospitals, residences for the elderly, and other institutions, were being served by 576 diocesan and 519 religious community priests, 401 brothers, and 4,378 sisters. There were 950 students in diocesan and religious community seminaries. An additional 14,480 students attended the local Catholic colleges and Saint Louis University; forty-three high schools educated 22,681 teenagers; 213 elementary schools had 88,786 pupils. The Parish School of Religion program, which began in 1962 for children attending public schools, was serving more than 20,000 young people. Twenty-seven religious communities of men and fifty-four of women operated within the archdiocese. The archdiocese had 2,136 sisters teaching in its schools, supplemented by 2,236 lay teachers. It was the high point of production in human terms in the history of the archdiocese.

However, times change. Forty years later the archdiocese has 377 diocesan priests, active and retired. There are 1,788 sisters serving, together with 372 priests and 143 brothers in religious communities. But the news is not all bad. Laypeople have assumed positions once occupied by religious and have become active on an unprecedented scale in parish and diocesan affairs. While the personnel profile has changed, for better or worse according to one's estimation, advancements have been made.

African Americans today play major roles in professional sports, entertainment, politics, education, and other professions. Catholics are expected to participate in any interdenominational project in St. Louis, be it with regard to immigration, fairness in hiring, neighborhood development, peace promotion, or any other social action issue that comes before the public. Interfaith Bible study and discussion groups abound, and people of differing religious beliefs are comfortable in sharing with each other. Our worship has been renewed with a new Lectionary and new music and vernacular prayer. Because there are more than 120 Catholic colleges and fifty Catholic universities in the United States, the Catholic population is the most educated of all denominations in the country.

Cardinal Ritter would be pleased with this American scene. It conveys so amply the fruits of his life's work. It exists in part because of his efforts.

We are all indebted to him for what he achieved as a faithful servant of the kingdom of God.

Bibliography

The author found the following works especially helpful:

Abbot, Walter M., S.J., ed., *The Documents of Vatican II*. New York: Guild Press, 1966.

Anderson, Floyd, ed., *Council Daybook, Vatican II, Session 3, Sept. 14 to Nov. 21, 1964*. Washington, DC: National Catholic Welfare Conference, 1965–1966.

Cochran, Thomas C., and Wayne Andrews, eds. *Concise Dictionary of American History*. New York: Charles Scribner's Sons, 1962.

Code, Joseph Bernard, *Dictionary of the American Hierarchy*. New York: Joseph F. Wagner, Inc., 1964.

Gillett, Henry Martin, *Famous Shrines of Our Lady*, vol. 1. Westminster, MD: The Newman Press, 1952.

Guilday, Peter, ed., *The National Pastorals of the American Hierarchy, 1792—1919*. Westminster, MD: The Newman Press, 1954.

Hughes, Catherine, R.S.C.J., *The Monk's Tale: A Biography of Godfrey Diekmann, O.S.B.* Collegeville, MN: Liturgical Press, 1991.

Johnson, James, *Men Who Made the Council*. South Bend, IN.: University of Notre Dame Press, 1964.

Kung, Hans, *The Council in Action: Theological Reflections on the Second Vatican Council*. Translated by Cecily Hastings. New York: Sheed and Ward, 1963.

Kung, Hans, *My Struggle for Freedom: Memoirs.* Translated by John Bowden. Grand Rapids, MI: William B. Eerdmans Publishing Company, 2003.

Proceedings of the National Liturgical Week 1942. Ferdinand, IN: The Benedictine Liturgical Conference, 1943.

Proceedings of the National Liturgical Week 1949, Sanctification of Sunday. Conception, MO: The Liturgical Conference, Conception, Missouri, 1949.

Proceedings of the Twenty-Fifth North American Liturgical Week 1964, The Challenge of the Council: Person, Parish, World. Washington, DC: The Litugical Conference, 1964.

Southern, David W., *John LaFarge and the Limits of Catholic Interracialism, 1911—1963.* Baton Rouge, LA: Louisiana State University Press, 1996.

von Galli, Mario, and Bernhard Moosbrugger, *The Council and the Future.* New York: McGraw-Hill, 1966.

Yzermans, Monsignor Vincent A., ed., *American Participation in the Second Vatican Council.* New York: Sheed & Ward, 1967.

Other Books
by the Author

Religious Views of President John F. Kennedy in His Own Words (St. Louis: B. Herder Book Company, 1965).

John F. Kennedy Talks to Young People. Compiled and edited by Nicholas Schneider and Natalie S. Rockhill (New York: Hawthorne Books, 1968).

The Life of John Cardinal Glennon, Archbishop of St. Louis (Liguori, MO: Liguori Publications, 1971).

To Burn with the Spirit of Christ: Daily Readings on the Role of the Laity in the Church from the Documents of Vatican II (Liguori, MO: Liguori Publications, 1971).

Famous Mexican Churches: What Church Architecture Evidences of the Faith-Life and Worship in Mexico, with Special Emphasis on the Colonial Period (St. Louis: Kenrick Seminary, 1975).

95 Temple Israel

errors
34
35
40
87
89